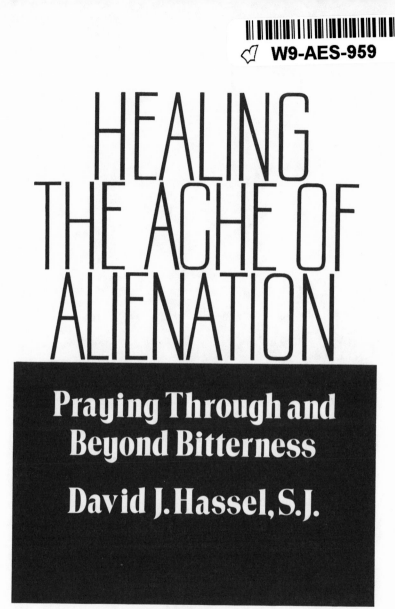

HEALING THE ACHE OF ALIENATION

Praying Through and Beyond Bitterness

David J. Hassel, S.J.

Paulist Press
New York/Mahwah

IMPRIMI POTEST
Robert A. Wild, S.J.
Provincial, Chicago Province of the Society of Jesus

Copyright © 1990 by
David J. Hassel, S.J.

Library of Congress Cataloging-in-Publication Data

Hassel, David J.
    Healing the ache of alienation: praying through and beyond
bitterness / by David J. Hassel.
        p.   cm.
    ISBN 0-8091-3126-9
        1. Spiritual life—Catholic authors.   2. Alienation (Theology)
3. Reconciliation—Religious aspects—Christianity.   4. Prayer.
I. Title.
BX2350.2H356   1990
248.8′6—dc20   89-38644
                                                                CIP

Published by Paulist Press
997 Macarthur Blvd.
Mahwah, N.J. 07430

Printed and bound in the
United States of America

Contents

Preface 1

Introduction: The Scene and the Meaning of
Alienation 5

One: Alienation from "My World" in Total
Distrust 15
[Trust Prayer]

Two: Work: Source of Alienation and
Solidarity 29
[Radical Prayer]

Three: Healing of Body and Spirit in Wisdom . . . 54
[Body-Wisdom Prayer]

Four: The Deepest Wound: Giving Up on
Oneself 69
[Reconciliation Prayer]

Five: Joseph of Nazareth's Alienation from
Mary 82
[Questioning-Wondering Prayer]

Six: The Loneliest Experience: Mid-Life
Divorce 92
[Frustration-Peace Prayer]

Seven: Smoldering Anger at God 110
[Anger Prayer]

Eight: The Joy of Hope: Response to
Alienation 138
[Trinity Prayer]

Epilogue: The Dynamics Between Types of
Alienation-Prayer 164

Appendix: Alienation Prayers in the Ignatian
Spiritual Exercises 168

Notes 170

"You yourselves were once alienated from him; you nourished hostility in your hearts because of your evil deeds. But now Christ has achieved reconciliation for you in his mortal body by dying so as to present you to God holy, free of reproach and blame. But you must hold fast to the faith" (St. Paul's Letter to the Colossians, 1:21–23).

"If anyone is in Christ, he is a new creation. The old order has passed away, now all is new. All this has been done by God, who has reconciled us to himself through Christ and has given us the ministry of reconciliation. . . . This makes us ambassadors for Christ" (St. Paul's Second Letter to the Corinthians, 5:17–20).

This book is dedicated to Fr. Edmund Fortman, S.J. and to Fr. Robert Harvanek, S.J. who have patiently and skillfully read and critiqued almost everything I have ever written.

Preface

Over the past twenty-five years I have been meeting many people undergoing alienation. By this I mean either a gradual distancing from others or a resultant perduring state of estrangement. Whether or not these people's actions occasioned this alienation, a majority of them were painfully pierced with feelings of guilt. Often this guilt was unwarranted; it was a false guilt having no basis in actual wrongdoing. Nevertheless, they felt a certain distancing, seemingly beyond their control, from co-workers, family, friends, country, church, and even God.

Such a process or an established state of alienation made them feel homeless somewhat like an alcoholic derelict or an orphaned child. This felt separation also angered and frustrated them, undermined their confidence, made them moody and erratic, even crippled a few. Much of this suffering seemed unnecessary. I felt that something should be done in addition to counseling; the something turned out to be spiritual direction and advance in prayer life. This book, then, is the result of working with alienated people who for a variety of reasons experienced themselves as cut off or distanced from previous pleasant situations and from people dear to them. Yet, as they came to accept their bitter feelings and loneliness, they discovered new ways to open their hearts to others and to God.

My own experiences of alienation also contribute to this book—despite my usual feeling of being very much at home and appreciated in the Society of Jesus. Because of spiteful hurt over what I deemed lack of respect for the work of younger teachers, I have never returned in thirty-five years to a high school where I first started teaching. It has taken me twenty years to return to a seminary where I taught enthusiastically and later felt my efforts wasted during the last year there. Three years ago I partially retired from academic affairs in order to write; it was a great relief from alienating frustration.

1

On two occasions I have felt fierce alienation from a Jesuit superior who I thought manipulated me and other fellow Jesuits.

Again, twenty years ago, after living for twelve months in what I experienced as a dyspeptic Jesuit community, I wondered whether this was the Society to which twenty-five years previously I had taken vows to the Lord. So, I know the feelings of bitter alienation. My estimate is that they had some basis in fact. Both feeling and fact, however, demanded a faith response which I hope I am giving even now some thirty-five to forty years later. As a result, I have personal experience as well as data from spiritual direction with which to encourage people to pray through and beyond the bitter feelings accompanying alienation.

What has helped me and others to face the guilt felt in alienation is the slow-dawning realization that one or other form of alienation is a common experience. Everyone experiences it somewhere in life. Then, too, the other side of alienation happens to be reconciliation. In fact, the Bible from Genesis to Revelation is the continuous story of alienation/reconciliation. It is not surprising, then, that prayer can be very helpful during and after one's experience of alienation. It gives perspective to one's skewed view of life, offers the close companionship of God to warm one's cold heart, and helps one to reach out to others with more confidence.

While writing the present book, I discovered that I had unknowingly been moving toward this theme in my previous books, *Radical Prayer* (1983, Paulist Press) and *Dark Intimacy* (1986, Paulist Press). The first book attempted to show how different forms of prayer eventually lead to intimacy with God and others. The second tried to describe how suffering can deepen and even enrich one's life as one enters more prayerfully into the daily life of God and his family, the church. In contrast, *Healing the Ache of Alienation* endeavors to sketch how intimacy, apparently lost through alienation, can be actually deepening through the very suffering of alienation. Such seemingly alienated intimacy can occur between marriage partners, friends, co-workers, and members of a family or religious group. It cuts between self and a once pleasant situation, and between self and God. This experience of seemingly lost intimacy can at times feel like the state of the damned since the pain can be excruciating, seemingly without end, and harshly accusatory of the loser. Thus the title: *Healing the Ache of Alienation.*

What is the aim of this book? First, to tentatively explore and to partially describe the way we experience the obscure intimacy of God in our various daily pains, especially those of alienation. A second aim is to sharpen awareness of how this obscure, yet immediate, presence of God permeates one's day. Third, I would hope that this book can bridge the gap between the contemporary Christian experience of God and that past language of spirituality which no longer touches our hearts. In this way we can benefit from our rich spiritual tradition which was expressed without the benefit of the sharp insights of social scientists and without the more recent discoveries of scripture scholars concerning the humanness of Christ. Thus terms like "original sin," "dryness in prayer," "abandonment to divine providence," "God's glory," "hope," "confession," "wisdom," "apostolate" and "kingdom" will be related to the more inclusive term "alienation."

In order to accomplish this triple task, each chapter ordinarily begins by discussing the *feeling* of alienation, that is, the hurt felt at the distancing from others and from one's own self. Next, it describes the *fact or source* of these feelings: the factual fissures in American society, in self, in family, in work, in country, and in church. Lastly, a *faith-response* to the particular facts and feelings of alienation is outlined. In it I try to highlight the type of prayer naturally issuing from the particular alienating situation—though the sociological, psychological and philosophical dimensions of this situation are not forgotten.

Among the people to whom I am grateful for all their help in writing this book, I would name first the people who had the courage to reveal to me the ravages of alienation in their lives and who thus gave me the strength to acknowledge my own. I am, of course, indebted to the administrators of Loyola University of Chicago whose grant of a research professorship made the writing of this book happen; they have without fail supported me strongly in any endeavor I proposed to them. The following people, most of them busy writers themselves, gave me incisive critique and steady encouragement: Edmund Fortman, S.J., Frank Oppenheim, S.J., and Robert Harvanek, S.J. I am specially indebted to John Dillon, S.J., for his painstaking review of the manuscript of this book during a time when his mother was dying. Fr. Peter Fox S.J. has more than once skillfully rescued my manuscript from computer-loss and damage. Other people who have guided me in certain portions of the book are gratefully mentioned in the footnotes.

Finally, the Cenacle Sisters of Warrenville, Illinois, provided me not only with a haven for writing but also with a hospitality for refreshing my spirit during the summer of 1988. I am indebted to them for good conversation and not a few challenging ideas. Then, too, my Jesuit community, as always, suffered my writing throes, but their humor, understanding and friendship kept me slightly sane. This was no small gift to me. Finally, may I also thank those various audiences who enlivened me with their interest and questions as I gave those talks which were to eventually become the chapters of this book.

David J. Hassel, S.J.
Loyola University of Chicago
Feast of St. Ignatius Loyola
July 31, 1989

Introduction: The Scene and the Meaning of Alienation

1. The Scene

To put it bluntly, America is rife with alienation and, therefore, to put it hopefully, she is ripe for reconciliation. In other words, our country contains many persons who are moving toward estrangement or are caught in a seemingly inescapable state of unwanted separation from others. Yet paradoxically, somewhat as in the beatitudes, God can work within our alienations to bring us closer to himself and to his people. This will happen, however, only if we are willing to be open-minded toward others and to suffer cooperation with the God who has lovingly fathered us all.

For alienation permeates us. Racism, not just black but also Jewish, Hispanic, and ethnic, painfully divides and distances us from one another. Divorce tears apart nearly half of our marriages so that bitterness alienates not only husband from wife but children from parents. Economic class-divisions based on wealth and consequent power are widening as the earning power of the lower middle-class diminishes and as the poor class finds its meager savings vanishing. Resentment between the elderly and the young is mounting because the elderly are thought to overtax the Social Security System and because the young are taking the jobs of those whose early retirement has been forced upon them. Further, the homeless stalk the streets of the large cities in growing numbers, perhaps two million nationwide, while for the first time whole families are living in urban shelters.

Internationally, in Africa, South America, and the Mideast, multiple wars have been stoking the fires of hate for a decade. Terrorism, the explosion coming from vast injustices suffered over the past century, ignites those countries of Europe and Asia which are still at peace. Meanwhile whole peoples from

5

Cambodia–Vietnam, Palestine, Ethiopia, Pakistan–India, and Central America are displaced from their beloved homelands. A more subtle divisiveness is spreading among the women of the world as they come to fuller awareness of how long they have been made into second class citizens of their countries and secondary members of their churches by the men of their culture and religion. All these foreign alienations, like pernicious seeds, are now windswept over the seas onto our American shores to add to our own home-grown variety of alienations— so shrunk is our modern world and so quickly affected is each country by the ills of surrounding nations.

This is the scene which confronts the Christian churches— a scene graphically portrayed in the Old and New Testaments and in the history of Christianity from Abraham to John Paul II. The Christ at the center of this panorama fittingly symbolizes alienation as he is hoisted up on the cross. Yet equally he symbolizes reconciliation as his crucified arms are stretched out wide toward the Father and toward his and our resurrection. This is why Christians hold Advent and Lent high in order to keep aware of all human alienations and of their potential for reconciliations. Perhaps this also explains why the Roman Catholic Church has introduced two new eucharistic prayers of reconciliation into its liturgy. Evidently contemporary Christians are becoming more alert to the lethal sickness of present-day alienation and are seeking to produce its only antidote: reconciliation.

2. Some Causes of Alienation

Robert Bellah et al., in their *Habits of the Heart*, lay the blame for American alienation on rank individualism. Bellah defines this attitude as the self-centered pursuit of the good life for the individual (success, power, wealth), for his family, and for a few friends without a sense of the common good of neighborhood, city and country.[1] Consumerism, the unrestrained buying of goods not really needed, is one aspect of individualism since it involves the wastage of things vitally needed by others, e.g. food for the third world nations. This selfishness, of course, spreads into how we do our work—sloppily, incompetently, irresponsibly—if we look merely to our own short-term pleasures.[2]

A second major cause of alienation is poor parenting. When both parents hold jobs, they come home tired and a bit impatient. So, they try to relax by watching television or by doing household tasks. To avoid tensions they tend to soften any disciplining of the children. As a result they tend to know their children less well. Naturally parents and children are more distant from each other and the ability of the children to socialize well out of a strong, warm family center is weakened. This makes the children more individualistic in their schooling, work, and later marriages. Alienation becomes "psychologically genetic."

This estrangement is compounded if the children receive a third-rate education. Lack of mathematical, writing, and reading skills makes it difficult for the student to find work in a technological society and renders the student bitter against parents, society, and self. Such polarization in civil society is mirrored in the church where people can take sides with vigor and later rancor about matters which they have studied and considered only superficially. Bridge builders are greatly needed to span the divisions among us.[3]

Subjective feelings throughout American society also play a major role in alienation. Prejudices against racial minorities, economic classes, religious groups, the elderly, the young and any other threatening group rise up like sturdy walls in this wide field of discontent. They split the country into seemingly genteel, yet secretly warring, factions. Then, too, the American penchant for concentrating on failures while giving less attention to successes and strengths heavily favors depression—a depression compounded by a dulled sense of gratitude for life and by a sharpened sense of being cheated in life. Other parts of this widespread depression are a cold loneliness because of family breakup at home ("no one seems to care if I live or die") and a felt loss of dignity because of heavy emphasis on roles and functions at work ("as though I'm just one more machine in an assembly line").

We are not only overwhelmed by the complexities of work, education, and culture but also discouraged at the scandal of immorality in business, government, and church, and especially in the personal lives of some friends, family members and local heroes. Alienation, then, can bring us to the state of social demoralization, a widespread feeling of helplessness to change what causes the disconnectedness or alienation of society.[4] Naturally, this produces rank individualism which is seen graphically in the lower percentage of those voting, in easy satisfaction with sloppy work, in nonchalant disloyalty toward family or team or company or church group.

3. The Meanings of Alienation

While describing the scenes and causes of this alienation, one can feel a bit lost in its vast landscape. So, perhaps, a definition of alienation would be welcome here: a felt distancing from others, self, work, and God. This is symbolized by the teenager wearing dark glasses, listening to walkman music and sealing any passer-by out of his tight little world. More scientifically George A. and Achilles Theodorson describe alienation in terms of

> a feeling of non-involvement in and estrangement from one's society and culture. The values and norms shared by others seem meaningless to the alienated individual. Thus he feels isolated and frustrated . . . unable to control his own destiny or to have a significant effect on the important events of the world through his actions.[5]

Here it should be stated that the alienation of which we speak in this book is not psychopathic, but rather is a normal part of everyday experience. It should not surprise the average person that he or she has moments, even days or months, of alienation. Events of life crash in on us; feelings of attraction and repulsion can happen before we know it and can last longer than we expected.[6]

Because alienation is a slippery term, it is important to nail down its varieties so that harmful misunderstandings can be avoided. Though such mounting on the "butterfly board" will tax the reader's patience, it will enable him or her to escape a more narrow understanding of alienation and to recognize the paradoxical richness of this life phenomenon.

First of all, there is such a thing as a healthy alienation. For example, the Old Testament prophets warned Israel that she would have to distance herself from the pagan style of life if she wished to remain Yahweh's bride. John the evangelist and the writer of the first letter of John, along with St. Paul, make it clear that Christians must move away from pagan worldliness and toward Christian life if they are to be united with God. Even in the twentieth century prophets like John Kavanaugh[7] and Archbishop Oscar Romero keep us alert to the need to distance ourselves from American pagan values. Romero's reminder is poignant:

> As long as the church preaches an eternal salvation without involving itself in the real problems of our world, the church is respected and praised and is even given privileges. But if it is faithful to its mission of denouncing the sin that puts many in misery, and if it proclaims the hope of a more just and human world, then it is persecuted and slandered and called subversive and Communist.[8]

This might be called biblical alienation, which seems quite in keeping with a pilgrim church.[9]

A second type of healthy alienation could be called contemplative. It is a temporary isolation from one's milieu or culture in order to understand it better by contrast and in order to return to it with new ideas and plans. An obvious example is to leave the United States to study China and its ancient culture. Or one could make a silent eight-day or thirty-day retreat so that one can understand at greater depth oneself, one's family and civic community, one's work-situation and the God who is presently providing for all of this. There are times when the artist, the writer, the sports star, the anchorite, and the poet must "get away from it all," must block out all distractions, if they are to concentrate on a dangerous leap beyond all previous accomplishments. Such contemplative alienation can occur when one is not afraid to be alone, silent, hungry, listening, and hoping like the Christ of the Judean desert. Distancing oneself from daily routines and familiar places allows one to perceive things in a new light and to readjust one's values and hopes.

But there are also unhealthy alienations such as letting oneself drift away from old friends ("They are always loading me with their problems"), from one's church ("It does nothing for me except raise the hackles of guilt"), from one's work ("There's little future there; why overwork?"), from one's favorite pastimes ("They take too much time and energy"). To gradually withdraw from such life-interests is to drift into an isolation resembling that of hell. Prideful independence is a second example of an unhealthy alienation. The self-made man or woman brags: "I don't need others; I can do it all myself." Or the ruthless Wall Street careerist can snap: "If others get in the way, it's their tough luck; this is a mean game and I intend to be the meanest in it." Then, too, what is revenge unless unhealthy alienation? After I have made sure by artful innuendoes that my enemy will never advance in our company and that his friends are isolated from any position of power, who will be my next victims and how will I ever be able to stop my lust for revenge? Executive-suite mayhem is quite a successful program for achieving the total isolation of unhealthy alienation.

Unfortunately, it is not enough to distinguish healthy and unhealthy alienations. It is necessary to distinguish alienation as objective historical fact and as subjective interior feeling. To confuse the last two is to make it impossible to become aware of the nature and extent of alienation. Objective alienation is the *fact* that the Cambodians are displaced and in exile from their homeland, the *fact* that the assembly-line worker is being frozen out of conversation by his fellow workers on the line, the *fact* that the Japanese bride is being sealed out of the family like an unwanted stranger by the groom's American parents, the *fact* that I am presently imprisoned for a misdemeanor.

On the other hand, the subjective interior feeling arising from the objective fact of alienation would be the Cambodians' sense of being helpless amid chaos, the assembly-line worker's feeling of cold isolation, the Japanese bride's horror at being rejected like an AIDS patient, and the prisoner's angry frustration at the bureaucratic machinery of courts and prison administrations.

Further, alienations can be unchosen or chosen and used altruistically or selfishly. When a person suddenly and unjustly is fired from his job as mail clerk but uses the time of unemployment to get to know his family better and to train himself for plumbing in order to support his family, he is undergoing an unchosen alienation and using it paradoxically as the occasion for closer union with his family, that is, for reconciliation. He could also use the unchosen alienation as an occasion for a new alienation of bitter unwarranted tirades against his family and the labor union. When another person leaves her family and friends to make a silent thirty-day retreat so that she will be a better doctor or fashion designer for others, this is a chosen alienation and altruistic. But when a man divorces his wife and family and goes to live in a foreign country in order to punish his family and to show disdain for his own nation (where he earned his fortune), this is a chosen alienation of mean selfishness.

All these distinctions about different kinds of alienation, healthy or unhealthy, fact or feeling, chosen or unchosen, altruistic or selfish, though presently boring to catalogue, will enable us later to avoid misunderstandings which can cause anguish or false guilt in our personal and business lives. For example, it is one thing to feel alienation from God or spouse; it is quite another thing if there is no historical fact causing the feeling of alienation. I do not have to experience guilt about feeling alienated from my God or spouse if there is no real fact of alienation. My spouse and my God still love me and I still love them despite my feelings of distance from them. On the other hand, if the feeling is generated by the fact that I have belittled my spouse in front of others or that I have treated God as just one more ornament in the universe, then I must take action to change the fact and thus dissolve my guilt feelings.

4. The Dynamics of Alienation

Alienation can spread like an infectious disease. The more I find myself factually separating from family, then from friends and finally from my work and church, the more I experience alienation from my own self. For these basic relationships contribute importantly to my sense of self which is now gradually becoming more susceptible to confusion and self-doubt as I lose touch with these significant people. I learn to criticize and even, on some days, to hate myself for all these alienations from others. Indeed, the more I experience alienation from the world and from myself, the more I feel alienated from the God who gave me this world and self. But this is to look at alienation merely as it works in and around the individual.

Alienation is also social. Insofar as the American and international scenes cause alienation because of deteriorating family life or individualistic business procedures or indiscriminate terrorism, they can affect my healthy sense of self the way toxic fumes from a deadly gas imperceptibly attack my otherwise healthy lungs and shorten my breath. This demoralization can separate me not only from my true self but also from others around me. Such social alienation brings me to distrust almost everyone around me and to feel deep doubts about the existence of a provident God. This can become a "cosmic alienation."

But there is a bright side to this black picture: alienation carries within it the potential for reconciliation. For the conflict and pain of alienation prompts me to seek out ways to relieve my suffering; this can yield insight into its causes and its remedies. I am liable to discover that the remedy needed lies in a process of reconciliation. One has only to glance at the most alienated of all men to understand this reversal. Christ experienced unchosen alienations from the Jewish hierarchy who systematically undermined his work, from the apostles who deserted him at Gethsemane, from the praetorium crowd who kept yelling "Crucify him," and from the Father who seemingly abandoned him ("My God, why have you forsaken me?").

But precisely within these alienations Christ was also reconciling the world. For he was to fashion his new church out of the repentance of the Pharisees-lawyers-priests who contrived his death, he was about to give the apostles who deserted him positions of leadership in this church despite their cowardly actions, he was intending to build the later church of Jerusalem out of the common Jewish people whom he cured of their ills but who did not defend him from death. And, astoundingly, he was now committing his spirit trustingly to the Father immediately after the cry "My God, why have you forsaken me?" How reconciliation can possibly happen out of the alienation process is the central theme of the following chapters.

Chapter One
Alienation from "My World"
in Total Distrust

1. The Feel of Alienation from the World

In describing here the feel of alienation, little attention will be given to the *fact* of alienation which may well cause the feeling. Nor will we be dealing with psychopathic alienation. Rather, our present intention is to explore everyday feelings of alienation which puzzle the average person whether the alienations be healthy or unhealthy, chosen or unchosen, selfish or altruistic.

What hurts most is feeling alienated from one's family. If a child is under constant criticism from a demanding parent or a jealous sibling, she will feel shrunken, even palsied—unlike the child who is expanded by praise and twists in delight at her mother's appreciation of the dandelion bouquet put in the center of the dining room table. The shrunken child feels the deep anger of frustration because "I can't please anybody." The adolescent who learns "to live by the rules or else" may conform for a while even as he envies his close friend whose trusting parents allow the latter spontaneity and some crazy antics. If he is a minister's son, he may feel violent temptations to do the wildest acts in order to shock the local congregation into recognizing his freedom to be himself and not just the minister's son shackled by adult expectations. Underneath the armor of conformity burns a constant rage. Naturally the child or adolescent feels guilty about the angers directed at the loved family, but he or she also feels a distance growing between the self and the family. The resultant confusion about family loyalty only makes the alienation more painful.

Later on in friendship or marriage, one hears oneself say: "I thought we had something going—something beautiful and lasting—now it seems empty of meaning, dead." Or a series of mounting misunderstandings ends up with the words: "Why did he have to say that—why did she have to do that?" Warm confidence has given way to a cold sense of betrayal.

Occasionally at the same time, the job which once lit up my life and filled me with blazing ambition now seems to offer me no excitement, no future. The interest I once shared with fellow teachers or lawyers or carpenters is gone. As I listlessly perform the job-routines with little desire to cooperate with others, bitterness creeps into the work atmosphere and I hear remarks such as "Jenny, you used to be so bright, so good at your work; what's happened?"

This disenchantment with or alienation from my work often is accompanied by boredom with the leisure activities which once brightened my weekends. Hobbies like guitar playing, hiking, watching professional football, swimming, tennis, stamp collecting, painting, all seem trivial and lifeless. Joy seems so distant from me. Like the restless St. Augustine who became angry at the contented laughter of a beggar, I start envying the joys of others. "I wish she'd stop smiling so much; it gets on my nerves. She has almost nothing; what right does she have to be so happy? Maybe she's too dumb to be unhappy."

This antagonism can spread over the whole American landscape. I resent that the USA is no longer first among nations in armament, business, industry, sports, and economic wealth. I wonder whether the local government is able to protect my rights as the newspapers uncover judges whose decisions have been bought and legislators who are owned by big businesses. I ask myself sarcastically: "Where is our so-called intelligent foreign policy taking us—into war and terrorist blackmail?" I sadly observe the polluted skies and lakes, the product of technology gone astray. Anger explodes in me at the use of computers to catch tax-dodgers like myself. This is the antagonism of widespread alienation in me.

It may be matched by a strong distrust of the vitality and flexibility of my church. She seems unable to cope with my or others' problems such as divorce, ecclesial bureaucracy, updating of attitudes toward science, the agony of the homeless, religious wars, sex dysfunctions, sharing of responsibility with the laity, and so on. Indeed, she is seemingly unable to provide me with a lively sacramental experience, a meaningful liturgy, a training in prayer. She does specialize, however, in disjointed, unprepared homilies and in off-key congregational singing.

When such resentful outrage, felt betrayal in marriage and friendship, disenchantment with one's job, boredom with hobbies, antagonism toward the whole American culture, and mistrust of the church are all working havoc in me, then surely I am alienated from "my world."

2. The Ache in Alienation

At the same time as the alienated person feels distanced from others, he or she experiences an ungovernable craving for family-ties, friends, cooperative work, the free-wheeling of hobbies and recreation, and the incorporation into something greater than the petty self, larger than its vision and hope. This constant throbbing desire in one's heart is the ache of alienation. It also contains a growing fear of total exclusion from community and a dread of that terrible loneliness which is a hell.

At times this energizes a desperate struggle to be accepted no matter what the cost in money, in subservience to others, and in loss of dignity.[1] At other times it may provoke angry violence, an almost paranoidal response. At still other times a faith-response will rise. At all times, however, one experiences the great void of not fitting anywhere, of being utterly homeless. The perduring ache at the center of one's being seems dark and forbidding even if it is one's own ache. For it engenders an icy chill of distrust toward everybody and everything. This becomes like a wall of ice protecting the alienated person from those who might hurt him or her. It promotes uneasy conversation, superficial exchanges of affection, and tight control of anything shared.

In reaction, in order to escape personal fragmentation, the alienated person searches for a center for his crumbling universe. This is instinctual, as I found out one day when talking with the mother of a five year old neighborhood terror who was busy in the backyard organizing all his playmates. Every once in a while, he would come storming into the living room, climb up on his mother's lap, wait for her to pat the back of his head while she continued talking with me, and then slip off her lap to take charge of affairs in the backyard. About every hour during our long conversation the procedure would be repeated. Slowly it dawned on me that he was simply reassuring himself at regular intervals that the center of the universe was still in the house and still loved him dearly. Such reassurance the alienated person wants with all his or her heart. It can be the rich source of reconciliation. But where find this center for one's shattered world? That is the haunting question.

In fact, the alienated person wants to be held tight by another person lest he or she fly apart. The hug means that someone cherishes us, that someone will live through the terrible night with us. I once saw this happen with a young married couple. The husband worked for an insurance company where he had been promoted past the level of his competence and where each day he was filled with the fear of making the final mistake and of being summarily fired for it. When he would return home at night, he would be exhausted. After a while, his wife interpreted his passivity to mean that he had lost interest in her and the children. Factually she was the center of his universe and her embrace was an escape from the jungle of his fears. Without her he would have broken into a hundred pieces. When she finally told him of her fear that he had grown indifferent to her, he could tell her of his daily fears and not worry that his story would frighten her. Their embrace that night set strong the center of their universe. They could face together that he would give up his job to take one paying less but located within his competence.

The ache of alienation carries within it the balm for its healing—but only if one intelligently reflects on it with someone who is not afraid to challenge as well as to console. Someone has to be at the center of one's universe.

3. The Faith Response to Alienation from the World

The basic faith response to alienation from the whole world is the act of trust arising out of the feeling of alienation itself.

One notes this in the Old Testament accounts of alienation. At Yahweh's call Abraham abandoned Ur-Haran, his ancestral home, to enter into a strange land. In the midst of this healthy chosen alienation "hoping against hope, Abraham believed and so became the father of many nations" (Rom 4:18). Thus he became the reconciler of all nations in being reconciled to Sarah's conceiving a new heir and to God's promise that he would be the father of all the uncircumcised. The experience of Joseph the patriarch is another instance of trust arising out of the alienation itself. Here Joseph endures the unchosen and unhealthy alienation of being sold into Egyptian slavery by his own brothers. Yet when years later the brothers turn to Egypt and reach out to the unrecognized Joseph for survival provisions, his compassionate rescue of them arises out of his longtime alienation from them. "I am your brother Joseph. . . . God sent me here ahead of you . . . to ensure for you a remnant on earth and to save your lives in an extraordinary deliverance. So it was not really you but God who had me come here; and he has made of me a father to Pharaoh" (Gen 45:4–8).

David's decision to number his people for more efficient taxation and military levies is a chosen, unhealthy alienation as it brings a plague upon his people. Still, David refuses, in the midst of this factual and felt alienation, to doubt the continuing love of Yahweh for him. Out of trust he forms a household of faith, becomes the forefather of Christ, and writes those trust-nourishing psalms which unite (reconcile) all Christians. Despite the bullying of his four "consolers," the brokenhearted Job puts his full trust in Yahweh's goodness, refuses to take on an alienating false guilt for sins never committed, and is commended by God for his brave honesty. During the Jewish people's exile in Babylon, Daniel describes their alienation and calls for reconciliation based on trust:

> We are reduced, O Lord, beyond any other nation, brought low everywhere in the world this day because of our sins. We have in our day no prince, prophet or leader, no holocaust, sacrifice, oblation, or incense, no place to offer first fruits, to find favor with you. But with contrite heart and humble spirit . . . we follow

you unreservedly; for those who trust in you cannot be put to shame (Dan 3:37).

It is not only the Old Testament which describes how trust brings reconciliation out of alienation. The New Testament life of Mary, the mother of Jesus, tells the same story. When at the annunciation Mary is "selected out" of all the daughters of Yahweh to be the mother of the messiah, she feels an accepted alienation and, with her fears, rushes to trustfully join Elizabeth and Zechariah's protective circle of affection. Although Joseph's doubts, now dispelled by the angel's reassurances, had temporarily separated Mary from him, now she trustingly joins him at his first invitation. The stinging refusal of her Bethlehem relatives to house her and Joseph is healed by her trust in the welcoming words of the shepherds. At the very time that she is presenting her son to be joined to the Jewish church, Simeon informs her: "This child is destined to be the downfall and the rise of many in Israel, a sign that will be opposed, and you yourself shall be pierced with a sword—so that the thoughts of many hearts may be laid bare" (Lk 2:34–35). The predicted alienation will nevertheless end in reconciliation if trustful sharing of thoughts and feelings is allowed.

The exile from the familiar Bethlehem environs to strange Egypt and to the Jewish enclave-community there demands trust that in this alien atmosphere Joseph can nevertheless provide for her and the child. More trust is needed when later Joseph decides to sequester them in the cramped atmosphere of Nazareth. Out of a subsiding panic at the loss of Jesus in the great Jerusalem temple, Mary says: "Son, why have you done this to us? You see that your father and I have been searching for you in sorrow." Then she hears the response typical of a twelve year old: "Did you not know that I had to be in my Father's house?" (Lk 2:48–49)—but she watches him, unlike the ordinary twelve year old, return to Nazareth in trusting obedience.

Mary also experiences apparent rebuffs at Cana when the wine runs low: "Lady, how does this concern of yours involve me? My hour has not yet come" (Jn 2:4–5), and at Capernaum when she and the family try to rescue Jesus from the crowds: "Who are my mother and my brothers? . . . Whoever does the will of God is brother and sister and mother to me" (Mk 3:33–35). But her trust remains even as, at Calvary, she is separated from her son and given to the apostle John to be protected: "'Lady, there is your son.' In turn he said to the disciple, 'There is your mother'" (Jn 19:26–27). Out of each alienation scene comes the call to deeper and deeper trust so that reconciliation can occur.

4. Prayer of Trust out of Alienation

The ultimate basis for escaping alienation from the world is faith in the ever-creating God's affection for us. But can we believe that the Lord takes delight in each of us and enjoys our company—despite all our tricks, manipulations of others, sins, shortcomings and occasional meanness? Is it true that I am only as alone as I want to be? How prove this to myself?

First of all, is it true that Christ took delight in each of his disciples and trusted them totally? Consider their first apostolic swing through Galilee which, despite their misgivings, turned out to be an astounding success. So, "Jesus rejoiced (Greek: his chest swelled in exultation) in the Holy Spirit and said: 'I offer you praise, Father, Lord of heaven and earth, because what you have hidden from the learned and the clever you have revealed to the merest children.'" On other occasions, he took them on short vacations to a deserted quiet spot away from everything so that he could chat undisturbed with them, cook a leisurely meal, play some games, laugh at their stories, and sing a bit—though on noteworthy occasions the throng would find him to hear his teaching, to be healed, and to live off the multiplied bread and fish. In fact, these disciples were his brothers as he told the Easter women: "Go and carry the news to my brothers that they are to go to Galilee, where they will see me" (Mt 28:10; Jn 20:17).

Fortunately for us, the disciples finally did believe in their brotherhood with Christ and they became different men. Thomas the apostle's "My Lord and my God" was spoken as he

gazed on the wounds of the human Christ and realized that this
was the price of brotherhood paid for his cynical self. How
could he and his life ever again be the same?

We, too, wonder about Christ's affection for us. Yet it is
nowhere more powerfully expressed than in the story of the
lost sheep: "I tell you, there will likewise be more joy in heaven
over one repentant sinner than over ninety-nine righteous people who have no need to repent" (Lk 15:7). Can I believe that
he looks forward to being with me, that he takes delight in me,
the sinner? It is very important that I so believe. Why? Because
the more I believe that God enjoys me and my companionship
the more security I feel. I now know what it means to say that
baptism has made me a born-winner—if I can trust God and his
church. All the other sacraments, too, are meant to be moments
of intimacy with Jesus, especially the eucharist where he literally melts into my whole being to strengthen me and to show
his affection for me. Is this not at least brotherhood or sisterhood with Christ?

Further, the greater my security here, the greater becomes
my apostolic strength and daring. For I am freed from worry
and am ready to do costly deeds for the Lord and his people.
Then the greater such strength in me, the larger my hopes grow
as I discover that God does not intend to waste one ounce of
my energy, one second of my life. Next, the greater this liberating hope in me, the greater my ability to sacrifice for others,
even for my enemies. Nothing gives me the enthusiasm to love
others as my enjoying one great love in my life. Just observe
how newlyweds love all things out of their one deep love. A
benevolent infection then occurs, since the more I love others,
the more delight I take in the Lord who is vitally present in
these others. In turn, the more actively I believe and live as the
brother or sister of Jesus, the greater becomes my desire to give
him joy. Is this not a convincing proof of our brotherhood or
sisterhood with Christ?

These are the reasons for saying that we are alone only as
much as we want to be. For is it not true that the more confident we are of being loved, the more confident we are of being
lovable and of being able to love others? Is this not the font of

all intimacy and reconciliation in the good husband or wife, among the children, with the single person, vowed or not vowed?

5. The Hero/Heroine of Trust: The "Old Shoe"

To see concretely how prayer of trust works out of alienation to restore such reconciliation and intimacy, it would be helpful to draw the profile of the "old shoe," the person in every community who literally holds it together. Ironically, as we shall see, this reconciler sometimes experiences alienation precisely as she or he heals a situation. The "old shoe":

(a) is always around for people and, therefore, is sometimes accused of not being productive;

(b) refuses to join cliques and to play favorites and therefore is lonely at times;

(c) builds bridges between groups and individuals and therefore occasionally gets stepped on from both sides;

(d) enjoys a remarkable prudence (more than shrewdness) and therefore people do not give her or him much time for self with their requests for advice in complicated situations;

(e) usually has a hopeful viewpoint and is therefore open to the charge of being pollyanna, wishy-washy;

(f) does not deal in abstract clichés or vast perspectives, but in folksy, down-to-earth stories—no matter how much education she or he has;

(g) sees both sides of controversial issues and can even argue either side effectively in order to clarify points of agreement and disagreement (yet is well aware of where his or her "vote" will go) and so is called two-faced by the community extremists;

(h) places a high value on friendship and camaraderie and therefore is considered a little soft by the heavily armored people;

(i) has a genially cynical sense of humor, that is, he or she enjoys human foibles yet respects the people exhibiting them; he or she is not unaware of original sin but has Chris-

tian hope in people; and so, some see the "old shoe" as cynical, even condescending.

Without the "old shoe," alienation can become somewhat
frightening, but with him or her, reconciliation becomes possible—though often enough at the expense of the "old shoe."

What is the secret of the "old shoe" who never gives up on
people and situations and who therefore can hold people and
things together with that patience which St. Paul so admired?
The secret is a hidden joy underlying all the "old shoe" does.
This joy seems to contain a persistent hope in that final reconciliation of all persons which is called the communion of saints.
This is the great community of today and tomorrow where we
will all find a final home and be deeply cherished.

A second element in this joy is a sharp awareness of the
Holy Spirit's presence in each person and in the whole family
of God, particularly the Christian church. "For if by the offense
of one man [Adam] all died, much more did the grace of God
[the Holy Spirit] and the gracious gift of the one man, Jesus
Christ, abound for all" (Rom 5:15). A third element seems to
be the *élan* of eliciting joy in others, that is, of forming Christ's
kingdom in down-to-earth events and ways. The "old shoe's
joy" says to all the world: "Yes, I am a sinner, perhaps a great
sinner, but my God is a God of forgiving reconciliation, not of
vengeful alienation; and this is how I see other people as also
dear to the Lord."

Such joy is the mark of the thoroughly Christian person.
Yet as Ladislaus Boros notes: "Joy can be the heaviest cross in
the life of a Christian. It is the testimony of the divine that costs
perhaps the greatest effort."[2] Rahner points out that Mary's life
was filled with the same anxieties, worries and hurts as our lives
carry—some few hours of supreme happiness along with many
routine hours of pains and cares.[3] Yet her daily secret joy is our
hope of being healed.

The persistent joy of Francis of Assisi, the great reconciler,
has endeared him to all, no matter their religion or type of atheism. Yet he made it a point to keep himself in spiritual joy by
immediately turning to prayer when tempted to dejection. He

had the lute played when he was in particular pain; at the other extreme he would burst into French song when the melody of his spirit was strong. He even rebuked sad-faced Franciscans because they depressed others. Finally in death he had the brothers sing to him as they wondered at his joy.[4] These joys surfaced at times out of the deeper joyful trust which he had in Christ's love for him and his love for Christ. But trust always includes painful tension; it exacts a price even though the accompanying joy is well worth the cost.

The prayer of trusting with its secret joy seems to be a powerful way of restoring reconciliation out of alienation. But as the Old Testament figures, the mother of God, and Francis of Assisi will attest, it is not an easy prayer. The profile of the "old shoe" lends itself to the same conclusion. Trust prayer stretches through all one's dealings with others as it seeks to heal wounds, to invigorate doubters, to stabilize rickety people, to elicit joy in the downcast, to mend friendships and communities, to bring beauty and verve into a sometimes tired old world and to keep the "old shoe" sane. Despite the sufferings involved, what prayer is more worthwhile and more life-giving?

6. Trust Prayer

Trust prayer is the prayer of day-to-day living through reconciliations and alienations, through the momentary ups and downs of the ordinary day. It is so basic that no techniques can lead into it since it founds all other types of prayer. For trust is what makes all prayer possible, is what starts and continues all prayer, is what first bridges between all humans and between humans and God. Consequently it carries the deepest meaning of life as the following story illustrates.

A priest friend once tried to help a person whom he called "the loneliest woman in the world." He had met her during his hospital rounds. The nurses had told him that in three weeks not a person had visited her, nor was there any mail for her. He soon found out why. When he inquired about her family she said: "I have nothing to do with them; all they do is bring me their boring problems and try to borrow money." Later he asked whether she liked her secretarial work. She answered: "The work is all right, but the people around me I can't stand. They gossip a lot and I'm sure they talk behind my back too. So, I don't give them the time of day." Later she added: "I don't trust anyone except my dog, Caesar. He's the only one who gives a damn about me." The priest said with a smile: "You trust God, don't you?" "I sure don't," she answered. "He's the one who got me into this mess and has left me in it. Even if he exists, I wouldn't bother myself to call on him for any help."

A few weeks later the priest visited the lonely woman in her apartment and said: "I came to see how you are after the hospital stay and to meet Caesar." She replied nonchalantly: "You're too late. He betrayed me too. He ran off for a few days last week and I had him put to sleep when he returned." With that she eyed the priest with utter disdain and he knew it was time to leave.

This negative example indicates what it means to say that trust is the ultimate foundation needed for even the slightest acquaintanceship, to say nothing of love and of prayer. This is why trust prayer cannot be directly taught; it can be learned only by osmosis from those who trust deeply and pray just as deeply. We cannot seal ourselves off from such people without dire results. In addition, because trust is so deep and delicate, it is the hardest thing to do. It demands a willingness not only to be vulnerable to others but simultaneously to be thoroughly self-respecting. One must know one's own value in order to surrender oneself in vulnerability to another person and especially to God. Otherwise one risks becoming either pompously self-assertive or mawkishly subservient.

Oscar Romero was a person who knew what it was to surrender to trust. He achieved a delicate balance of vulnerability and of self-respect in his trust of God and of others—but at no small cost. Archbishop Romero was not at first noted for his work for the poor. That was why the wealthy power-group had no objections to his being made archbishop of San Salvador. He would cause no disturbance outside his cathedral. But after Romero viewed the body of Rutilio Grande, S.J., his friend, torn by bullets from high-powered rifles fired from ambush, he saw that his life could never be the same. Grande had been killed because he had tried to organize the poor farmers of El Salvador against the vast injustices of the landowners. These campesinos were Romero's own sons and daughters, and he now took on their cause—though he well knew it would likely mean his own violent death.

From then on, every day found him speaking out to and for the poor, urging the power bloc to stop their violence, meeting with anyone who would be interested in protecting his poor, and visiting any threatened family or village. It was a matter of course that he be shot just after delivering a homily in honor of the mother of a journalist-friend whose newspaper had been bombed two weeks earlier.[5] Out of his own self-respect and out of his love for Christ's kingdom, Romero had taken on the vulnerability of his people because he trusted in them and in Christ.

Not only is trust, because it contains the deepest meaning of life, quite difficult to do. But also its depths take a whole lifetime to learn. A priest friend at eighty years old had suddenly been struck by swiftly moving loss of sight. Being a voracious reader, a "shrewd observer of the passing scene," and something of a water-color artist, his darkening vision put him into a deep melancholy. He could not believe that God would allow this to happen to him after all he had been through as a missionary superior in Shanghai cleverly fending off the Japanese occupying forces and later the triumphant Red army. After expulsion from China, he had been greeted in the USA by more demanding work as superior of his order's national seminary and later as the order's American provincial.

So, he asked God, "Have I not kept my sense of humor and won the admiration of my brother religious even while updating the order against some fierce opposition? Then why let this happen to me?" But the trust he had shown the Lord and others all through the previous years of danger and tension began to resurface slowly. His angry frustration began to subside, he found recording devices to gather the information and to experience the pleasure which reading had once given him, he learned to listen more intently to others, he developed the ability to relive his best memories, he became more reflective and prayerful. The trusting attitude of many years had outlasted the time of depression and reasserted itself.

Thus trust prayer grows slowly through the years, event by event. It is a constant experiencing of vulnerability in ever new facets of one's personality. But it is also a slow maturing of one's self-respect by which one gains the ability to respectfully trust others. Just as such trust grows in a long-developing friendship, so, too, does trust prayer grow almost imperceptibly. Only after comparing five- or ten-year periods of one's life can the decline or increase of trust be recognized and measured. So, too, trust prayer.

When the young woman, Mary of Nazareth, said to the Lord's messenger: "Let it be done; I am the Lord's servant," she made a tremendous act of trust. Yet this was only the beginning, grand as it was. From then on she had to grow in this trust if she was to do trust prayer up to and far beyond the time of her son's crucifixion. At times she, like us, must have felt that her ability to cope with the challenges of her new role was quite inadequate. But somehow she was empowered to continue trusting in herself almost as much as she trusted the Lord who allowed her to enter dangerous situations. This trust in her own trust may well have been the Lord's finest gift to her during her life on earth. Can our prayer of trust be based on such a gift? Why not?

Chapter Two
Work: Source of Alienation and Solidarity

One of the most devastating experiences is to feel alienated from one's work. Life seems empty. The self feels worthless. There is relief only when the day's labor is over. But next morning comes the great dread as one faces the brutal ugliness of returning to work. The alienated worker wonders whether others have noted his or her listlessness at work—especially the employer. Anger lurks beneath the surface, ready to flare up at the slightest provocation. Retirement is not the answer when one needs money for next month's payments on the house, car, and credit cards. Suicide, however, becomes more understandable. Such alienation comes in at least three forms: disenchantment with work, workaholism, and a sense of being overwhelmed by one's job.

1. Three Types of Work-Alienation

A. *Disenchantment*

Disenchantment means that I no longer find my work meaningful. I am not climbing toward some beautiful distant peak. Rather, my work is pivoting around the same center like a small, dismal merry-go-round which is slowing down and giving out discordant music more and more weakly. My work gives me no excitement, no sense of accomplishment, no promise of a brighter future. I cannot understand the enthusiasm of fellow workers as they do their boring routines, while I cannot wait till Friday, 5 P.M. My bitterness grows when the employer remarks that the quality of my work has gone down and when co-workers leave me more and more alone.

When I return home in the evening, my once favorite hobbies of novel reading and soft rock music seem utterly trivial and lifeless. The bitterness spreads toward a son who seems ungrateful, toward a lifelong friend who tells me "to buck up and quit thinking of myself so much," toward the supermarket which always seems to be jacking up the prices when I arrive to buy groceries, toward the politicians who seem to have so many answers to problems that never go away, toward my church which seems to be always urging me to do something for the social outcasts.

Yet at the same time there is in me an ungovernable craving to do cooperative work, to succeed in something, to find relaxation and joy in free-wheeling hobbies, to be part of something greater than myself. I try to escape into the fantasy world of the local bar. Or I find solace in home TV. There with the remote control in hand I am omnipotent, and with the expected comfort of the six-pack I am temporarily relieved of ennui occasioned by all the problems of family, work, self, church, and country. I may even attempt escapist prayer such as "Lord, take me out of this place; let me die, the sooner the better."[1]

B. Workaholism

Workaholism seems to be the direct opposite of disenchantment with work. Yet it is equally isolating and eventually dreadful. Workaholism is the attitude whereby I put success in my work ahead of all other values such as home, health, God, country, spouse and children. It is the individualism of the self-made man or woman who wants to do it all by himself or herself. Put simply it is careerism: "My family and friends have to learn to live with my ambitions. After all, I do support them well even if I'm gone a lot and am somewhat distracted when I'm with them. If God wants me to take care of my family and have a little joy in life, then he'd better be satisfied with the shortened Sunday eucharist and my quick night prayers."

The workaholic is adept at stitching together clichés in defense of her or his attitude: "Keeping busy is the only way to stay healthy and normal. Watching the cash value of my work and even of acquaintanceships is necessary for getting due respect for myself. A person is worth precisely what he accomplishes in life; no other way to be remembered after you've left the scene. You have to drive fast in the race of life; otherwise you end up breathing everybody else's exhaust fumes. As for prayer, it has to pay off in getting me what I need and in giving me a little peace and consolation along the way so that I can do my job. Otherwise, it's a waste of precious time needed for my work. God needs us to succeed if he wants us to have decent family life and a strong church."

The workaholic cannot find time to read or hear: "Like vapor only are man's restless pursuits; he heaps up stores and knows not who will use them" (Ps 39:7). Even more disturbing would be: "It is vain for you [the workaholic] to rise early, or put off your rest, you that eat hard-earned bread, for he gives to his beloved in sleep" (Ps 127:2). The workaholic forgets the parable of the eleventh-hour workers to whom the Lord gives the same pay as the first-hour laborers (Mt 20:1–16). At this point the workaholic accuses the psalmist (perhaps even Christ) of not appreciating hard work and the world built by heavy labor. He or she forgets that David the psalmist was a kingdom builder and that Christ's public life was an almost continuous whirl of activities.

There is a difference, however, between these "achievers" and the workaholic. David and Christ appreciated: "I busy not myself with great things, nor with things too sublime for me. Nay, rather, I have stilled and quieted my soul like a weaned child . . . on its mother's lap" (Ps 131:1–2). Both knew how to seclude themselves in order to sink deeply into the God for whom they were laboring. But how does the workaholic explain that his or her work supposedly done for God has become more important than God? How does the workaholic show God (who labors daily to keep the universe in existence and to give it ever greater beauty) that it was foolish for him to take the seventh day off to enjoy his world? How indicate to him that Sunday work is necessary to our culture and that it is unrealistic to ask us to set aside time to enjoy our family, friends and Christ?

Perhaps, in response, a few questions could be put to the workaholic: Do you realize that your behavior is an obsessive compulsive mechanism, not an heroic activity? Do you recognize that through your accomplishments you are trying to prove to others your worth, your very lovability? Are you not trying to extort from others some appreciation of your work and thus of yourself? Would they not rightly refuse to be impressed at your large salary and position of power? Are you not haunted by the need to prove and reprove your personal value?

C. The Worker Paralyzed by the Complexity of His World

If the disenchanted worker feels empty and the workaholic feels very full of self and its accomplishments, there is another person who feels paralyzed by the overwhelming size of the organization for whom he or she works. The paralyzed one is literally haunted by a sense of powerlessness in the face of a complex business or entertainment enterprise or medical world. The person feels like a scrawny pygmy alongside such mammoth duties. At midnight these fears torture his or her sleepless mind: "Who am I to cope with the mighty General Motors or the Sears Financial Network or the state government or the U.S. Army or the Actors Equity Guild? What difference does any good deed or even an honest life make amid the corruption I meet each day? Look at what happened to those who tried to fight Mr. Big. My job and my life have become too complicated; they're crushing me."

Does all this sound unreal? Then consider J.C. Haughey's report of the varied work-motivations in members of a Catholic business guild gathered to explore the meaning of their various jobs:

(1) my job is only to provide means to support the family; it has little or no intrinsic worth;

(2) only with luck does work yield any meaning—though my co-workers are nice people;

(3) I pay off for my sins with my work; I earn my life by the sweat of my brow;

(4) work is first of all for self-expression, then for financial support, finally for the communal good;

(5) God has called me to my specific job; here I share in his creativity and serve the way Christ did.[2]

Has the worker, paralyzed by his own insignificance before the intricacies of modern life, forgotten or disbelieved St. Paul? Paul, too, felt at times overwhelmed by the job which Christ had given him:

> I willingly boast of my weaknesses, that the power of Christ may rest upon me. Therefore I am content with weakness, with mistreatment, with distress, with persecutions and difficulties for the sake of Christ; for when I am powerless, it is then that I am strong (2 Cor 12:9–10).

Why is this so? Because "we do indeed live in the body but we do not wage war with human resources. The weapons of our warfare are not merely human. They possess God's power for the destruction of strongholds" (2 Cor 10:3–4). Without this conviction, Paul could not have evangelized the whole Mediterranean basin. Nor could Ignatius Loyola have sent out his men to become the renaissance-educators of seventeenth and eighteenth century Europe. Nor could Vincent de Paul have taken it on himself to organize the royal court to rescue the destitute of France's urban centers and the galley convicts of the French navy. Nor could Frances Cabrini and Madeleine Sophie Barat have spanned the world with their foundations for the sick and the uneducated. These men and women would agree with Paul: "In all that we do we strive to present ourselves as ministers of God, acting with patient endurance amid trials, difficulties . . . we seem to have nothing but everything is ours" (2 Cor 6:4–10).

2. Reconciliation Is Solidarity Through Our Work

The single response to disenchantment with work, to workaholism, and to paralysis before cultural complexity is solidarity with God and with others through work. Solidarity is more than

mere cooperation, though it must start with this. It is cooperation based on respect for self and for others and on a sense of
the worthwhileness of each person's contribution to the common enterprise whether, for example, I am a janitor for the university or the dean of faculties or a student or a part-time
teacher. I saw this exemplified by a worker at St. Louis University's Cupples House, a beautiful residence of matched
wooden flooring and gracefully cascading staircases. I asked the
janitor whether doing the same work every day bored him. He
shook his head and explained why not. "When I have your
meeting room shining clean, all the chairs arranged in a nice
semi-circle, the ashtrays sparkling and ready to hand, and the
lights bright, you have a better meeting, don't you? That better
meeting goes up to the dean or president and he makes better
plans, no? And the whole university is better, right? That's why
I ain't bored ever." And with that he took the small glass of
Scotch I had poured for him after the meeting and put it on the
top shelf of a closet. There was to be no drinking on the job.

Solidarity, if we pursue it, can reconcile us from our alienations. But it requires cooperation with God, co-workers, management, and church in a mysticism of service based on clear
priorities and on the refusal to be "just busy." What all this
means will become clearer as we reconsider disenchantment,
workaholism and paralyzing fear at work. It will demand a
Copernican revolution against the popular pagan work-ethic.
This we will see in exploring disenchantment with work.

A. *The Disenchanted Worker and Solidarity*

First of all, it should be clear that the Lord has decided to
work through us in the salvation process. In this way we learn
to serve others, later express love for them, and finally find God
in them—as many a dedicated lawyer, transport worker, nurse,
or sports star has found. In addition, one cannot labor loyally
without discovering one's talents, limitations, and good and bad
attitudes. The stresses of failure or the joys of success in the
emergency room, the jet-liner cockpit, or the classroom reveal
the deepest secrets of one's personality to oneself. Indeed,

through this self-knowledge one comes to patiently understand one's co-workers, to realistically form a team and sometimes to establish lifelong friendships.

At the same time I must keep in mind that this sharing of work is not simply with co-workers but also with God. In fact, I am sharing in *his* work, not he in mine. He is the senior part- ner who invites me to work with him in making the world more gracious and beautiful and then commissions me to my job— especially by way of my loyalty or obedience to the communal good. This commission is, of course, not a binding duty but a privilege. Paul's explanation of church-unity applies also to the solidarity of each person's workday since the same God works differently in all of us at all times and places: "We, though many, are one body in Christ and individually members one of another. We have gifts that differ according to the favor bestowed on each of us" (Rom 12:5-6). And this is God's work which we do in solidarity: "There is but one body and one Spirit, just as there is but one hope given all of you by your call. There is one Lord, one faith, one baptism; one God and Father of all, who is over all and works through all and is in all" (Eph 4:4-6).

Furthermore, the work of each is unique cooperation with God and others; no one else can do it:

> There are different gifts but the same Spirit, there are different ministries but the same Lord, there are dif- ferent works but the same God who accomplishes all of them in everyone. To each person the manifestation of the Spirit is given for the common good. . . . But it is one and the same Spirit who produces all these gifts, distributing them to each as he wills. . . . God has set each member of the body in the place he wanted it to be. . . . Even those members of the body which seem less important are in fact indispensable (1 Cor 12:4- 22).

Nor is any personal action wasted but each is woven into the fabric of the kingdom. For "as often as you did it for one of my least brothers, you did it for me" (Mt 25:40). Again, this is done according to one's talents and with unexpectedly large reward: "He called in his servants and handed his funds over to them according to each man's abilities. . . .After a long absence, the master of these servants came home and settled accounts with them. . . . 'Since you were dependable in a small matter I will put you in charge of larger affairs'" (Mt 25:14–21). In addition, Christ does not waste even our failures, drawing good for us out of each one, if we allow him to do so. "He comforts us in all our afflictions and thus enables us to comfort those who are in trouble, with the same consolation we have received from him. As we have shared much in the suffering of Christ, so through Christ do we share abundantly in his consolation" (2 Cor 1:4–5).

Nor does he waste our sins, but uses them as occasions for instructing us and for showing his affection for us. Is this not the meaning of the lost sheep, the prodigal son, Zacchaeus' call, and the forgiveness offered to Mary Magdalene? Is this not what strengthened St. Paul: "We know that God makes all things work together for the good of those who have been called. . . . If God is for us who can be against us? . . . Who will separate us from the love of Christ? Trial, or distress, or persecution, or hunger, or nakedness, or danger, or the sword?" (Rom 8:28–35). Here is the personal healing needed for Christian solidarity with God and others precisely through our work. What could be more soothing to the ache of alienation in each of us? What can give us surer hope?

With the Lord's words ringing in our ears, we should also recall that he depends on our shepherding his flock only as long as he wants to. Individualistic ambition is ugly in his eyes and he will protect us from it. Ezekiel trumpets this fact to the shepherd-leaders of Israel:

> Because my shepherds did not look after my sheep,
> but pastured themselves and did not pasture my sheep
> . . . I myself will look after and tend my sheep. . . . I
> will rescue them from every place where they were
> scattered . . . the lost I will seek out, the strayed I will

bring back, the injured I will bind up, the sick I will heal, shepherding them rightly (Ez 34:8–16).

Further, the Lord depends on our work only in the way and at the time he wishes. He is the Lord of creation and work: "Learn then that I, I alone, am God, and there is no god besides me. It is I who bring both death and life, I who inflict wounds and heal them, and from my hand there is no rescue" (Dt 32:39). In other words, this is the Lord's world, not that of Marx or Freud or Darwin or Nietzsche or Einstein. He is the one who gathers our works and ourselves into solidarity with each other and with himself in order to lessen our disenchantment with work. No one else can do this: "Let not the wise man glory in his wisdom, nor the strong man glory in his strength, nor the rich man glory in his riches. But, rather, let him who glories, glory in this, that in his prudence he knows me, knows that I, the Lord, bring about kindness, justice and uprightness on the earth" (Jer 9:22–23).

Solidarity with the church is also vital for dissipating this disenchantment and replacing it with a sense of worthwhileness. Vatican II's *Constitution on the Church in the Modern World* insists that "Christ, to be sure, gave his church no proper mission in the political, economic, or social order," but on the other hand the church recognizes

> an evolution toward unity, a process of wholesome socialization and of association in civic and economic realms. For the promotion of unity belongs to the innermost nature of the church, since she is by her relationship with Christ, both a sacramental sign and an instrument of intimate union with God, and of the unity of all mankind.[3]

In thus promoting unity or solidarity at all levels of society and among all the various human roles in the development of world culture, the church promotes meaning in the lives of all people. For it is the failure to see any unity or any progress toward unity which instills the disenchantment with one's work or role in life. Hence the meaning and value of one's work can be enhanced by this vision of genuine unification or dynamic solidarity.

At the same time, the church stresses the unique contribution of each person to this unification. The Vatican II document, *The Decree on the Apostolate of the Laity*, declares:

> In the church, there is a diversity of service but unity of purpose. Christ conferred on the apostles and their successors the duty of teaching, sanctifying and ruling in his name and power. But the laity, too, share in the priestly, prophetic, and royal office of Christ and therefore have their own role to play in the mission of the whole people of God in the church and in the world.

If one objects that this sharing is quite subordinate to the hierarchy's leadership, the fathers of the council respond that lay people

> exercise a genuine apostolate by their activity on behalf of bringing the gospel and holiness to men, and on behalf of penetrating and perfecting the temporal sphere of things through the spirit of the gospel. . . . It is proper to the layman's state in life for him to spend his days in the midst of the world and of secular transactions . . . as a kind of leaven.[4]

Thus the roles of the hierarchy and of laypeople are distinguished, not to isolate them but to better unite them in close cooperation out of their distinct autonomies. This is the solidarity of reconciliation, the unity of the church interiorly within itself and exteriorly with the world through its members.

One can note seven steps by which lay people, along with the religious and the hierarchy, can mediate and thus gradually bring the church into solidarity with the whole world:

1. The church, here meaning the bishops, the theologians, and the lay intelligentsia, does not attempt to think for all lay

people, but does assist them theologically in their thinking as she challenges them to take leadership in and outside the church.

2. The church as a whole calls all lay people to holiness amid the complexity of their work and the value-conflicts within their culture.

3. The hierarchy offers more active roles in the liturgy of the eucharist and in all parish organizations.

4. Lay people become more aware that Christian creativity is exercised not merely at home but also in the 9 to 5 job.

5. Lay people more aggressively help the church to face basic societal issues of family stability, business integrity, armament control, women's dignity, and so on.

6. Lay people unite the church more closely with the world through their civic leadership in key positions of government, entertainment, business, education, labor unions, and armed forces where they live Christian values boldly.

7. Lay people, now well educated and influential in all sectors of society, begin to build a more Christian American culture. Thus, through trial and error, they inventively find ways to integrate Christian living and teaching with newly developing areas where Christ's teaching has not yet been formulated, e.g. genetic engineering, business "takeovers," third world economic assistance, the hosting of displaced peoples, and so on.[5]

In this way, the more that Christians achieve solidarity among themselves and in their work, the more Christianity itself is brought into solidarity with the world of which it is a part.

John Paul II, in his talk to the bishops at the seminary of Our Lady, Queen of the Angels, in Los Angeles on September 16, 1987, commented on the above seventh step:

> Primarily through her laity, the church is in a position to exercise great influence upon American culture. . . . But how is the American culture evolving today? Does it clearly reflect Christian inspiration? Your music, your poetry and art, your drama, your painting and sculpture, the literature that you are producing—are

all those things which reflect that soul of a nation being influenced by the spirit of Christ for the perfection of humanity?[6]

So, the solidarity among co-workers when united to solidarity with the church is expected to influence a new solidarity of Christianity with the American culture. Would this be sufficient to lessen disenchantment with one's work and to replace it with a realistic vision of how one's work and oneself fit uniquely into the advance of the Christian people toward God?

B. *The Workaholic and Solidarity*

Then there are the busy people—too busy to let God into their work by breathing an occasional prayer, too busy to find time for the eucharist and the sacrament of reconciliation. They are hypnotized by the lure of success. The good life consists mainly in getting ahead of others. This is the alienation of gross individualism, of arrogant self-centeredness, with its destructive undermining of solidarity.

There are some basic facts, however, which sometimes help the workaholic if he or she has time to consider them:

1. God loved me *first* before I could do a single thing for him or for others. That is why God created me instead of others; I am personally attractive to him and have his affection. "If I take the wings of the dawn, if I settle at the farthest limits of the sea, even there your hand shall guide me and your right hand hold me fast . . . you have formed my inmost being; you knit me in my mother's womb. I give you thanks that I am fearfully, wonderfully made" (Ps 139:9–10, 13–14).

2. So, God values me first and only secondarily my work. If he has to choose between them, he would invariably choose me first no matter how important my work for others and for the church. In contrast to the apostles' hot ambition to be first in the kingdom, Jesus embraced a little child who had never done a moment's work (Mk 9:33–37). Then a bit later he associates this action with his third prediction of the pas-

sion, his seemingly useless death on the cross. Almost immediately after this, he tastes the bitterness of John's and
James' bold request to occupy the seats of power on his
right and his left when he comes in his glory (Mk 10:32–
41). Ambition already clouds the clear priority just
enunciated.

3. There are no professional apostles. For the Lord does most
of the work in my accomplishments. I am simply the amateur apprentice whom he privileges to work with him. I cannot afford to forget, as did the rich young man, that "Many
who are first shall come last, and the last shall come first"
(Mk 10:31).

4. God's plans may be better than mine, better for me and for
others, because as my lover he wants only the best for me
and for the people whom I try to serve. Yet do I not still fear
that he will change my plans if I confide them to him? "If
anyone of you thinks he is wise in a worldly way, he had
better become a fool . . . for the wisdom of this world is
absurdity with God" (1 Cor 3:18–19).

If these facts are clear to me, then why do I continue to
keep so busy that I find time only for my work, not for God and
others? Have I muddled my priorities? For example, do I want
to please every requester so that I never say "no" lest they
think me selfish? Do I equate being Christlike with being an
unfailingly "nice person"? As the Rev. G. Niederauer contends: "Jesus said 'no' whenever he had to do so in order to
continue his lifelong 'yes' to the Father's loving will."[7] He said
"no" to the man wanting to first bury his father, to Martha asking him to tell her sister to help her, to those wanting him to
stay longer in their town, to the Gadarene demoniac wishing to
go with him in the boat, to those demanding a miracle of him
to prove his messiahship, to those requesting that he have his
disciples fast the way they did. Does finding time for others, by
occasionally saying "no" to constant work-demands, eventually
provide the leisure for solidarity? Would this reveal workaholic
busyness to be an isolating compulsion which guarantees my
future loneliness?

Again, what keeps us from having time for friends, family, and God so that intimacy may become possible for us? In other words, are we so frantically using the technology of telephone, car, computer, television, jet transportation (all ironically meant to give us more leisure) so that we can run always faster to keep up with the ever more rapidly changing world? Are we and our culture in danger of careening out of control?[8] Is this where the solidarity of mutual trust, of common vision, of leisurely family life and of cooperative work is most needed so that one can deal with the individualism of accelerating workaholism?

This attitude, of course, does not mean that we try to avoid all occasions of tension. Tensions are part of life-growth. Christ's tensions were not momentary and small: "I have a baptism [of sufferings] to receive. What anguish I feel till it is over. Do you think that I have come to establish peace on the earth? I assure you the contrary is true" (Lk 12:50–51). He exhibited more than one outburst from tension: "What an unbelieving lot you are. How much longer must I remain with you? How long can I endure you?" (Mk 9:19; see also Mt 15:17; 16:7; Mk 7:18; 8:17–19).

These tensions were signaled in his remark while crossing the Cedron valley: "My heart is filled with sorrow to the point of death" (Mk 14:34) and they culminated in the bloody sweat of Gethsemane (Lk 22:44). Yet amid all the tensions, Jesus found time for vacations with the apostles, time for Matthew's party, time to visit Martha, Mary and Lazarus, time to bless children, time to speak with Nicodemus late into the night. He would not let the tensions of sheer workaholism rob him of the solidarity of intimacy with his co-workers, his friends, and chance acquaintances.

C. *Solidarity and Being Overwhelmed by the Complex World*

Just as with disenchantment and workaholism, the alienation felt at being overwhelmed by the wide scope and heavy responsibilities of one's work is nothing new in the experience of God's people. The church's response in terms of solidarity with God and one's co-workers is based on Hebrew tradition.

The first social legislation in all human history was Moses' law for immediate payment to the day laborer. This solidarity with the day worker was strong because, unlike the Greeks and Romans, the Hebrews saw both the necessity and the dignity of manual work. It was God's command: "By the sweat of your face shall you get bread to eat" (Gen 3:19). So, each doctor of the law, like each of the patriarchs and the prophets, had a speciality such as farming, wood cutting, charcoal burning, vine tending, shoe making, even grave digging. Indeed, Jesus and the apostles were handy men, artisans, fishermen, tent-makers and tax clerks. This Hebrew custom had a leveling effect on the natural hierarchy of middle managers and wealthy owners presiding over the workers. The solidarity of a common understanding and goal for work could effect mutual justice among these three societal classes.

In Christ's time, in order to protect workers, rabbis set the conditions of their work-hours, housing, pay, clothing and feeding, and determined their obligations of respect and faithful service to the employer.[9] The Hebrews' vision of work as a mandated co-creating with God enabled them to be peaceful when confronted with the complexities of the Roman culture. God was working with them; how could they lose—even if they did not understand everything?

A modern rendition of this traditional solidarity with God and others is found in John Paul II's *Laborem Exercens.* There four basic revolutionary principles are given for building solidarity between management and the worker and for assuring a consequent solidarity with God:

1. Work is meant *more* to perfect the person as the image of God than to change the world by improving it. Yet to complete God's creation by work is man's charge: "God created man in his image; in the divine image he created him; male and female he created them. God blessed them, saying: be fertile and multiply, fill the earth and subdue it" (Gen 1:27–28). This means that cultural and technological progress

should not perversely make one less human by enslaving one to itself, nor should it alienate a person in fear from the society for whom he or she works. Instead, it should help the person to reach fuller manhood or womanhood and thus image God better.

2. The person doing the work, not the type of work done (e.g. menial), determines the value of the work. Otherwise, the worker is turned into an instrument of the work (a human machine) rather than the work remaining subordinate to the human. For the material result of the work has no ultimate value, but the human person is ultimate value. This reverses the workaholic understanding and use of labor. It establishes that technocracy is what crushes the worker's sense of dignity under its demands for total dedication to its complex processes apart from his family and religious life.

3. Capital resources (e.g. tools, machines, profits) are to be at the service of the worker. A person's labor, because constitutive of his or her very being, is always the primary value, whereas capital, being merely a tool of labor, is to be at the service of labor. Thus the disenchanted worker has meaning for his or her every task. No longer is reaching for maximum profit at the expense of the laborer's working conditions and wages to be considered "good business." The common good is to be the directing principle of solidarity among humans and with God. In this the disenchanted worker discovers self-worth and the ultimate meaning of his or her work.

4. Work as a cooperative venture produces solidarity (vs. alienation) since it thereby unites workers into unions, management into organizations, consumers into associations— all three of which are meant to be united for the common good of a nation.[10]

Such solidarity, since it is a sharing of responsibilities, enables the person overwhelmed with the intricacies of modern work-life to be more sure of his worth and his place in society.[11] Solidarity, however, is as costly as it is beautiful. It demands strong discipline to sacrifice for the common good, e.g. by improving working conditions at the expense of large dividends for stockholders. It is not always easy to do menial work with pride in it and in oneself when the culture looks down upon menial work. Nor does one quickly refuse to misuse another person when one's own economic success (e.g. maximum profit derived from below-standard wages) is at stake. When building bridges between warring factions, the person dedicated to solidarity knows that neither side will be happy with his or her efforts.

Solidarity is still beautiful, however, because it puts people first—ahead of possessions, riches, and comforts. This engenders mutual respect, lowers tensions and establishes peaceful procedures. The result can be increased patriotism and the basis for a growing solidarity with God.

Solidarity, then, can actually be an implicit mysticism of sevice wherein we find God present within our endeavors to make other people's lives more humane. In this service is a secret joy, at once a strength for the present and a hope for the future—"We seem to have nothing, yet everything is ours" (2 Cor 6:10). This is illustrated in John the evangelist's introduction to the passion (13:3–6) which builds up dramatically to what seems a most disappointing let-down:

> Jesus—fully aware that he had come from God and was going to God, the Father who had handed everything over to him—rose from the meal and took off his cloak. He picked up a towel and tied it around himself. Then he poured water into a basin and began to wash his disciples' feet and dry them with the towel he had around him.

With this unexpected action of a slave, Jesus showed himself to be the servant of the servants of God. The insignificant act of a slave became equal to the noblest act of death for the beloved ones. It would not have occurred unless Jesus had experienced, within himself and amid complex conflict, the secret joy of the Father's approval of this act of service and unless he had seen the joy of being loved in the eyes of his apostles.

In the eyes of Thomas Aquinas, this mutual joy in lover and beloved is especially powerful in the love of friendship which goes beyond the love of desire (to love something for what it gives me) and the love of benevolence (to love out of duty). For with the love of friendship the lover identifies fully with the beloved. Whatever touches the beloved touches and affects the lover: "The life I live now is not my own; Christ is living in me" (Gal 2:20). This intimate union or solidarity with Christ inevitably breaks out into concern for others from the inmost circle of friends and family to the outermost circle of the whole world.[12] Thus the solidarity of serving others leads to union with Christ which reciprocally leads into deeper solidarity with others in a benevolent circle of growth. In this way the fearsome complexity of the world can be domesticated into the family of God and made more benevolent.

The person who is overwhelmed and paralyzed by the complexity of his responsibilities in serving others might well take to heart St. Paul's response to his problem: "God chose those whom the world considers absurd to shame the wise, he singled out the weak of this world to shame the strong . . . so that mankind can do no boasting before God. God it is who has given you life in Christ Jesus. He has made him our wisdom" (1 Cor 1:27–30). Not satisfied with this, Paul adds later: "And so I willingly boast of my weaknesses instead, that the power of Christ may rest upon me . . . for when I am powerless, it is then that I am strong" (1 Cor 12:9–10). This is the paradoxical mysticism of service which makes the weak strong, the absurd wise, the leader a servant, in enhancing the kingdom of God. It is also the dynamism of that Christian solidarity which is meant to heal all alienations, especially those involving disenchantment, workaholism, and paralysis of endeavor. At this juncture, however, one might ask: "But what is the source of this mysticism of service?" One important response would be "radical prayer."

3. Awareness of Radical Prayer Means Solidarity/ Reconciliation

There is a basic type of prayer, always implicit and hidden, which quietly and powerfully energizes the mysticism of service and thus generates the solidarity of workers among themselves and with society, church, and God.[13] This radical prayer must be described in different ways, so many are its faces and so subtle is its presence. Of the eleven descriptions given below perhaps only two or three will illuminate its presence within a particular person's prayer-experience, and each person will find a different combination of descriptions. This is due to the fact that the experience of radical prayer is beyond the imaginative and conceptual at a fourth and deepest level of praying. Let us consider these eleven descriptions, starting with the one using four levels of experience.

A. *Eleven Sides of Radical Prayer*

1. Here radical prayer is a quasi-direct experience of God (an obscure intimacy with him) below three previous levels of experience which are:

1st: becoming attentive to God by way of vocal prayers, aspirations, thoughts expressing insights, conversations with God;

2nd: feeling God fitfully without words: emotionally knowing God, consoled by strong images (rock, fountain, sunset, gentle wind, mighty storm, child's face, tears of a man);

3rd: grounding one's convictions (which put God first among all values) and living this out frequently and explicitly in concrete, everyday actions; thus experiencing the strength-hope-peace of God amid defeat, suffering, exhaustion; and hence contemplating in action.

Underlying these three levels of prayer lies a fourth level:
being intent on God beyond words, thoughts, feelings, images, convictions, sufferings, joys, yet at the same time living within these, so that one is simultaneously intent on God and on his people as beloved by him.[14] In this way does solidarity become as real as the one praying and as real as his or her affective and effective actions.

This last level may be the actuation of the fundamental option for God[15] as well as the radical source of all solidarity with God and his people. The great temptation here is to neglect this level or form of prayer for previous levels or forms in which one feels more at home. For in this fourth level one cannot readily calibrate progress. Nor can one easily find adequate spiritual direction for it because of its quiet darkness which is the obscure immediacy of God. This is true even though the prayer at this level is actually enriching and directing prayer in the upper three levels. Unfortunately, to revert to the previous levels simply because one feels more comfortable there is to risk routinization, stagnation and occasionally even despair of prayer.

Additional Ways of Experiencing This Radical Prayer Are:

2. a tending to the presence of God, a tender reaching out to God; an attitudinal leaning toward God, a submissive listening to him amid commonplace duties, work, and joys.[16] "Teach me your paths, guide me in your truth and teach me, for you are God my savior, and for you I wait all the day" (Ps 25:4–5). "For what do I wait, O Lord? In you is my hope" (Ps 39:8).
3. a hungering/thirsting for God, sometimes piercing; a continuous stretching into the dark unknown beyond all knowing to a seemingly pure nothing which is actually a great stark presence luring one on from depth to depth, to depth.[17] This search manifests itself as a driving desire to recognize the nothingness of all but God.[18] "God, you are my God whom I seek; for you my flesh pines and my soul thirsts, like the earth, parched, lifeless and without water" (Ps 63:2).
4. a quiet stripping away of all the praying person's false ambitions, techniques for "successful" prayer, pride of accomplishment, pettiness, many former "certitudes," and the vanity of being "dependent on no one." It is a becoming sensitive to one's dark emptiness in which one discovers the Trinity's presence within oneself, the presence underlying all consolations and desolations, the presence powering all one's actions.

5. a steady hoping (secret joy) in Christ, the Lord of history, who is running the world; the lessening of anxiety and the increasing of a perduring tranquillity about present and future problems. "Only in God be at rest, my soul, for from him comes my hope. He only is my rock . . . I shall not be disturbed" (Ps 62:6–7).

6. a simple presenting of oneself to God as he works wonders within the self—something like two people on a long auto trip quietly letting their friendship grow by osmosis as they silently observe the passing countryside from different viewpoints or something like my retired father telling my mother to quit washing the breakfast dishes and to come and sit in the living room with him while he continued reading the sports section avidly and said nothing to her.

7. an ongoing discernment which enters into every decision, big and small, as though by a divine instinct (Karl Rahner's gifts of the Holy Spirit? or the reason why Ignatius Loyola spoke of making the examen of consciousness seven times per day?).

8. a floating along in the great underground river of God (fourth level of prayer) according to a particular focus such as a vigil light, a crucifix, a sentence from a psalm, the striking advice of a friend, an art work, a mandala; surrendering control and letting the divine current carry one along in the boat of prayer.[19]

9. a gentle revealing of how superficial is one's faith, how self-aggrandizing one's apostolic zeal, how condescending one's attitude toward God's family, how sentimental one's love for others—insights which would never have occurred, never been accepted, unless one were at a deeper level of faith, zeal, humility, and love.

10. at the same time a simple trusting that each event of one's day is chosen carefully and affectionately by Christ so that one can say to him: "I leave 'the when-where-how-what' completely up to you because I know for sure that you want only the best for me."

11. steadily thanking God for each life event and for the people in each event, while at the same time experiencing an

all-encompassing desire to let God be first in all one does ("For whom else would I do this job, counsel this person, suffer this humiliation? No one else would dare ask this of me").

Radical prayer, then, is twenty-four-hour prayer touching into all the happenings and people of one's day and night. It is "not dreaming . . . not reminiscing . . . it means getting in touch with who I am as the person who has had an experience and offering that 'who' to God . . . it is extremely common among people who ironically condemn themselves for not praying."[20]

B. *Measuring This Simple Radical Presence of God*[21]

It sounds a bit like blasphemy to speak of measuring God's obscure immediacy in our lives. Yet the need is there to discover whether we are kidding ourselves about his influence in our daily living. So, with trepidation I offer some six points of measurement, taking for granted that one is roughly comparing large periods like five or ten years of his or her life:

1. a renewed feel (zeal) for apostolic action shown in
   (a) a sharper awareness of Christ's presence in the words and actions of others; a fuller empathy even for those persons intensely disliked.
   (b) a greater freedom to accept minor and major disasters, a more relaxed sense of humor, since in God's world we are born-winners by baptism.
   (c) greater daring and willingness to "go it alone," if this be necessary, when something needs doing or saying; and yet a more strongly felt need for the companionship of teamwork so that the righteousness of zealotry is avoided. This translates into more humility.
   (d) stronger conviction that one's work is what the Lord wants and so a steadier drive to achieve it as obedience and events allow. In other words, liberation from attachments is occurring.
   (e) stronger hope that something good can come out of failure and more alertness to how God orchestrates acci-

dental events into a striking advantage for oneself or others.

(f) brief experiences of God's penetrating presence during breaks in one's work routines, e.g. short waits at the telephone or on the assembly line, walking between work areas, waiting in line at the local supermarket, driving the expressway. These act as stimulants to one's work.

2. a growth in self-knowledge ("Five years ago I would have been as angry as a hornet; ten years ago I would have given up on this impossible job"). This lets me know my limits more clearly and thus enables me to better recognize the Lord's power carrying me beyond my limits in writing a book, parenting a family, teaching a class, directing a labor bargaining session and so on. There is less fear here of being exposed for my weaknesses or crazy antics.

3. more sensitive to nature, music, beauty of face, nobility of action, grandeur of architecture.

4. more alertness to others, willing to listen more often and more acutely, sensing better the dignity and needs of others, stronger hoping in their goodness, greater desire to do secret acts of kindness for them.

5. more gratitude for the small events of life, for the hard scramble up the mountainsides even though occasionally sliding back down (e.g. alcoholism, lost friendship, illness, a muffed opportunity).

6. more readiness for God's will entering one's cherished plans, more desire to give joy to Christ's heart in all things, not so easily irritated or upset by people, by unexpected events, by sudden storms, by God's seeming aloofness from one's life.

When this radical prayer grows as the six criteria indicate, it builds solidarity because it breathes into our lives intimacy with God and hence intimacy with others. It is by far the most powerful element in alerting this world of ours to the permeating kingdom of Christ. But how is this dynamic prayer of God's obscure immediacy related to formal prayer? Does it enable us to dispense with the more explicit formal prayer?

C. The Role of Formal Prayer in Radical Prayer

What precisely is formal prayer? It is an explicit concentration (vs. the implicit awareness in radical prayer) of mind, heart and will upon God through vocal prayer, meditation, imaginative contemplation, aspirations, liturgical prayer, and so on. Usually it is done in a secluded spot away from the marketplace for a definite time each day. Even though intermittently formal prayer may appear to be mechanical, routinized, formalized and dust-dry, still it continually enriches radical prayer. Formal prayer is like isometric exercises which appear to have no result at the time but develop one's strength to deal with real-life efforts. Consequently, after a person has gone through thirty minutes of distractions, he or she still feels that "something good has happened" and that the formal prayer is worthwhile, even though to prove this seems quite impossible.

Why does formal prayer feel worthwhile even when it is almost boring? There are at least six reasons for this.

1. It gives new insight from time to time (e.g. through prayer of reminiscence or prayer of Christ's memories) to illuminate radical prayer.
2. It levels our pride as we struggle with distractions, dryness, sloth and fatigue; in fact, it establishes our solidarity with fellow sinners.
3. It alerts us when we drift away from God-consciousness in our everyday life because the very hollowness of formal prayer may occasionally be a sign for the praying person that his or her spiritual life is growing slack. Thus formal prayer often is the litmus test for good radical prayer.
4. It increases the sensitivity of the underlying radical prayer to God's world and to God. One learns to find God hiding within people and threading all events into the great tapestry of life.
5. It brings us to appreciate radical prayer as one breathes in God and calls his name aloud at the upper levels of prayer experience and then hears the name sounding more deeply at the center of one's being.

6. It pulses within radical prayer (long after the formal prayer period is completed) in the way that the chorus of a poem underlies the stanzas as they are recited or in the way that a friend's chance, but penetrating, remark echoes all through the events of a day.

Formal prayer, then, plays an important role within radical prayer so that the latter can be a rich source of solidarity with God and with others. Consequently, radical prayer can gradually heal us when we are bitterly disenchanted with our work or inhumanly workaholic at it or paralyzed by its complexities. Solidarity gives the self-esteem so needed in these days of cynicism if one is to confidently alert one's co-workers to the kingdom of God within and outside them.

Chapter Three
Healing of Body and Spirit
in Wisdom

All three synoptic gospels (Mk 5:1–20; Mt 8:28–34; Lk 8:26–37) describe the episode of the Gadarene demoniac, so important was this scene considered by the early church. The man had lived among the tombs, gashing his body with rocks as though it were another hostile being to be attacked. Day and night he had cried out against the townspeople, against God, against himself. Now, in spite of himself, driven by some strange attraction, he was rushing down the beach to meet Jesus whose boat had just reached the shore. He shouted: "Don't torment me." Then swiftly Jesus freed him from the legion of devils, restored his sanity, clothed him, had him sit in with the brethren, and lastly commissioned him to proclaim the Lord's deed throughout the ten cities.

The Gadarene's newly found tranquillity was the end of his self-hate. His exile from home and humanity was ended with his commission to spread the good news among the ten cities. Once feeling terribly alienated from God by his sins, his failures, his compulsions and his fears, now he experienced reconciliation with himself and God. But the townspeople whose pig herds had been lost and who were shocked at the recovery and reconciliation of the demoniac invited Jesus to leave. He had disturbed their prosperous ways; they preferred to keep him at a safe distance. The reconciliation of the demoniac had become the occasion for their chosen alienation from Christ.

No one of us is secure from demonic existence. We all have the inner experience of alienation from our own selves. It may start with loss of confidence in one's skills ("I used to be so good at handling people and at organizing my work; now I seem to get on people's nerves and muddle the simplest situation"). Then one comes to question one's motives for doing good ("I guess I'm simply a manipulator from way back; whom am I trying to impress? How much envy of others' successes enters into my ambition to be a first rate doctor or executive?"). Next arises a crippling awareness of one's sins, meanness, smallness ("Where did I learn that dirty trick? I thought I had grown up enough not to cheat, not to take advantage of people's weaknesses? Who would want me as a friend?"). One's consciousness is darkened by a profound sense of having wasted one's life ("Always the playgirl, I guess") or of having squandered precious opportunities never again to be offered: a prized job, a potential spouse, a friendship.

Later, one discovers a sense of the self disintegrating, as it sprays itself out in frantic activity, as it lurches through the day like a directionless drunk ("When will I ever get it all together like Henry or Alice? Am I to be the forever adolescent? Can anybody trust me?"). Lastly guilt covers one like a great overcoat which pulls tighter the more one struggles to get it off. The future will never be different from one's sin-laden past. The self is sure that it is undeserving of any person's attention, care, or affection. At this point violence against self and others becomes probable.

This alienation process makes a person feel like an outside observer of herself and her actions ("I am not really living in myself anymore"). There are two selves: the outside one is the prosecuting attorney, the inside one is the defendant. The prosecuting attorney, carping twenty-four hours per day, cannot be silenced: "You'll never change, so quit struggling; there you go bragging again like a four-year old; you've fumbled once more; you're incapable of doing a good job—admit it." Yet all this while the accused experiences a strong hunger for self-confidence, for the healing of her torn self, for the wholesomeness of a decently successful life. There is still an implicit hope, not yet completely crushed out, of reconciliation with herself and hence with others and with God. What is this hope? Let us explore for it within the very alienation felt from our body and from our spirit.

1. Body Prayer amid Alienation from the Body[1]

All of us who are overweight and addicted to food know what it means to lose respect for our bodies, our personal appearance. By not exercising properly we begin to lose control over the body so that it becomes like heavy baggage. Power to achieve is diminished; laziness begins to move through the body like a drug. To recapture lost exuberance, alcohol is used; besides, it momentarily dulls the pain from festering problems in family and at work. Yet it also disrupts normal patterns of eating, sleeping, and relaxing, further depleting our energies. We disown our tired bodies, hide our anger at people's demands upon us, and use violence on the body to get work done despite headaches, nausea, and frequent dozing. We are tempted to serve others frantically without thought of leisure if only to escape ourselves—so that "burnout," the loss of even reserve energies, occurs. We have succeeded in thoroughly hating our bodies even if each body is incarnate wisdom to be carefully listened to.

Further, we resent the limitations imposed on us by our bodies and are tempted to consider them as strangers to our selves. Flu may keep us from work or play and leave us weak. Arthritis severely limits our movement. Or our nerves respond slowly or fumblingly to crucial needs like avoiding an oncoming person or like pouring medicine without a spill. The aging process sharpens awareness of time's quick passing precisely when we must sleep longer, react more slowly, become less productive. The spirit seems to be imprisoned by the body as it struggles to express itself through the body but finds its wit muffled by slower speech or its exuberance masked by awkward action or its knowledge cramped by memory loss or its attention to the beloved wavering because of inability to concentrate.

At this point we may find ourselves resenting the parents who gave us defective genes, the God who brought us into an existence which is bodily, and the people around us who seem too busy to pay us much regard. We can forget that these limitations may also come from neglect of the body, the rejection of grace, and the failure to practice virtue—all of which would have allowed the soul to better penetrate and direct the body. Another mentality is needed to lift us out of our despondence. We are desperate for hope.

If we disrespecters of the body were to recall St. Augustine's dictum: "The life of the body is the soul but the life of the soul is God," we might give some consideration to the body's dignity. For the human body roots us deeply into the universe. Each one of us is the present confluence of thousands of years of genetic heritage and is the focal point for all the energies of the whole present universe. We build the world's future as we construct dams, plant orchards, sow fields and gardens, invent communication systems, erect mighty buildings, travel space, and work on assembly lines.

The body even enables us to lift the universe into spiritual living beyond the limitations of the body. We laboriously raise families capable of sacrificial compassion. We teach, preach and poetically create, by the sweat of our brows, what stimulates the human mind and heart to seek a fuller beauty beyond the merely material. Indeed, because the human body compenetrates the human spirit, it can express the spirit's nobility in dance, sport, and death for another. The human body reveals its closeness to God in liturgy, in heroic acts, in drama, and in the joy of creative art. One can even venture to say that the human body is an expression of God since Christ's bodily resurrection directly revealed the presence and care of God not only for Christ's body but for the body of each of us.

The human body, then, images God in his glory, carries the living promise (grace) of its immortality. Further, it is becoming more and more present to the whole universe as communications improve, space travel becomes real, and science penetrates into the deepest secrets of the universe. St. Paul sums this up: "This treasure [the glory of God shining on the face of Christ] we possess in earthen vessels to make it clear that its surpassing power comes from God and not from us. . . . Continually we carry about in our bodies the dying of Jesus, so that in our bodies the life of Jesus may be revealed in our mortal flesh" (2 Cor 4:7–10). Thus we image God and Christ in all our bodily actions. Even our death throes reveal the life of Christ vibrant not only in our pleasures and exaltations but also in our bodily sufferings and disappointments.

For these reasons, body-prayer with Christ is particularly able to reduce alienation from our bodies and hence from our spirits.[2] The purpose of this prayer is to get away from too much vocal, mental and affective prayer and to achieve a new liberty of expression, a new expansion of prayer-consciousness. This prayer is useful, then, when one is mentally tired and emotionally drained. Like the body it has three dimensions.

The first dimension is to use the body alone as symbolic expression of one's spirit, of one's attitude toward God. There are to be no words, no thinking of great thoughts, no heaving of sighs. One simply stands like the pentecostals with hands up and open to receive from the Lord. Or one kneels like St. Francis of Assisi with arms reaching out to the tabernacle or to the sunny sky to greet the Lord as one does in welcoming a friend at the airport. Like the Jewish people, one can sway the whole standing body in the slow rhythm of God's warming presence, or like David before the ark, one can dance one's joy or sorrow while offering any gracefulness of body or awkwardness of affliction to God. Some people stretch out their arms to parallel Christ's embrace of the world on his cross; others spread-eagle their body face down in the anawim's helplessness before God. Even the yawning mouth can symbolize one's emptiness, one's need to be fed like the small bird in the nest.

A second dimension of bodily prayer is to add the voice to bodily gesture such as saying from the anawim position: "My God, my God, why have you left me an orphan?" Bodily prayer can be groaning loudly in one's dryness, anger, frustration, desolation, or fear. It can be simple repetitive songs such as "Heal me, Spirit of the Living God," or singing along with a taped medley. It can be a laughing out in prayer as one recognizes humor in the gospel story or in a recent event at the auto repair shop. It is not being afraid to cry, even to sob, when one needs the Lord's warmth for one's coldness.

Then the third dimension of this prayer is using both body and voice to act out a prayer. This is not merely contemplating or thinking actions while sitting or kneeling; it is actually moving the torso, arms, legs, and head in a scenario. For example, walk with Mary and Joseph to Bethlehem; at Mary's invitation pick up the Christ child from the straw, hold him, kiss him on the forehead. On another occasion, stand in back of Christ as he does a sabbath healing of the woman bent double, take her elbow as she straightens up surprised, step back again to hear the tirade of the synagogue leader and try to avoid Christ's flailing arms as he angrily replies, later guide the cured woman back to the women's place in the synagogue (Lk 13:10–17). One person I know opens the door to invite Christ into his room and asks him to sit in the chair across from himself while he challenges Christ about events of the previous day and pauses to be counseled. At times there will be laughter, at other times quiet chagrin or even a few tears.

Such bodily prayer may leave us feeling awkward at first as though we were stage acting. Then is the time to ask God to make this prayer real. "The Spirit too helps us in our weakness, for we do not know how to pray as we ought; but the Spirit himself makes intercession for us with groanings which cannot be expressed in speech" (Rom 8:26). We have to patiently learn to adjust to this experience like the astronauts who in a laboratory setting simulating conditions of space travel learn to live with the experience of weightlessness. Patient trying brings surprises because the risen Christ is in us directing our three-dimensional prayer. It is not a private fabrication of the gospel since the word is just as present to the twentieth century as to the first one and the gospel is much more action than printed pages or thoughts (cf. Rom 1:16; 1 Thes 2:13).

Indeed, St. Ignatius went to the holy land amid fierce dangers to be able to walk, sit, touch, and sleep where Jesus had been. He needed to know exactly in what direction the supposed imprints of Christ's feet were set in the stone of the ascension. This was not antiquarian curiosity; rather, Ignatius wanted his body to be in tune with the rhythm of Christ's body risen and active in the sixteenth century. Is this being "mystical" or is it being fully human? Is it better to be inactive and bored rather than being more alive and joy-filled? Could this prayer, then, be a partial answer to a person's alienation from his or her body?

2. Contemplations and Alienations from the Human Spirit

The "midlife crisis" (from 35 to 55 years old), referred to by some psychologists, seems to be a form of alienation from the spirit which happens to young people also, for example, when facing the early death of a parent or of a younger school friend.[3] This crisis seems to happen most powerfully in elderly people who have not yet honestly faced their imminent death or the inevitable diminishment of their powers. Because the midlife crisis forces us to look at the ultimate values and hopes of life, it can be seen positively as a wisdom process, not merely as a fearsome prospect.

Raymond Studzinski, O.S.B. has profiled both the anguishes experienced by those undergoing "midlife crisis" and the bits of wisdom derived from these sufferings—bits of wisdom which can coalesce into a balanced view of self and life beyond petty alienations.[4] He finds that nine crucial experiences of midlife lead us to wisdom or bitterness, to reconciliation with or alienation from the spirit.

1. "Time is running out": dramatized by unexpected illness, death of parents, slowness of success, struggle with paunches and wrinkles, heavy responsibilities seemingly unending—in contrast with the American emphasis on youth, vigor, carefreeness, and living in the express lane. In reaction, a person may begin to dress and act like younger people in order to set the clock back but soon feels older, more angry at young people, more dissatisfied with self. If he reluctantly but realistically starts to appreciate his gifts of experience, skills, and friendship—garnered over the years and unavailable as yet to the young—he may escape bitterness and become more mellow.

2. "Am I really that bad?": expressed in a frantic attempt to do a lot beyond one's abilities, in a not too subtle envy of others' successes (even those of friends), in chagrin at lost opportunities or at one's own bungling, in a temptation to say "Oh, what's the use" and to give up. If the person can revise her dream of life, settle for a lesser success than previously hoped for and accept her limitations prudently (although probably with some melancholy), then she lowers the burners of frustration and moves toward the wisdom of realistic self-knowledge. The rediscovery of limitations need not level or isolate this person in alienation.

3. "I can beat these other people out; I've got what it takes": results in a new search for adulation and acclaim in areas outside one's competence (e.g. changing jobs rapidly, divorce and a new try at marriage, recognition for philanthropic leadership). It can mean a clinging to power even at the cost of friendship or of the business enterprise. Wisdom here consists in dismantling the false personality-myth, in admitting one's sense of inferiority, and in giving up careerism for becoming a useful, more hidden member of some larger group like the church, the interracial society, the businessmen's task force for training the unemployed. Such reestablished solidarity is wise reconciliation.

4. "You may call me an extremist but I'm usually right": returns a person to a less mature integration of his youth where the single clear idea is not to be qualified by other considerations. Conflicting dichotomies are enthusiastically pursued such as youth vs. old, poor vs. rich, masculine vs. feminine, boldness vs. timidity, autonomy vs. obedience, independence vs. attachment. Such zealotry, such failure to integrate opposites, makes a person irritable at the complexity of life and spurs violent attempts to simplify it (e.g. family moves from urban life to farming community with little preparation, quick divorce is attempted, refusal to pay taxes is adamant, all the poor are deemed shiftless and the rich worthy of careful cultivation). Such a person, racing along this smooth downhill road, is headed for solitary madness.

 If, however, he can switch off to the difficult uphill road where people of different ways of life cooperate in intellectual give-and-take and in respect for each other's convictions, then he may finally reach the haven of sane prudence. On this road one accomplishes the impossible of thinking young in an aging body, of listening to others (even when in a high state of creativity), of putting friendship ahead of career and of stressing life more than possessions. Solidarity or reconciliation of spirit proves that wisdom is operative.

5. "A person has to cut corners to make it in this world": signifies the conflict of personal with commercial values as one moves up the organizational ladder of success. One's press-

ing responsibilities always knit the cloak used to cover up the dirty tricks of the trade. But the camouflage wears thin and the executive or actress or marine colonel begins to hate himself or herself for knuckling under to financial and social pressures. The sane strategy is to try to better the organization despite its corruption and to be faithful to one's personal ideals no matter what the financial loss. The gaining of wisdom is not only painful; it is heroic at times.

6. "Does everything have to be changing at once?": can be a stubborn refusal to adapt to changing times, health, family needs, technological advances, a more realistic future. Trying to do "business as usual" while the business falls in shambles around one is to end up bitterly blaming everyone else for the fiasco which was avoidable only by restructuring one's methods and life. The wise reaction is to take significant time out to reconsider one's business methods and personal life. The resultant revision of all one's relationships will be intensely painful but also fruitful in peaceful reconciliation.

7. "I must get control of everything if I'm to survive": is the basic recipe for losing all control. Facing economic loss, the casual independence of one's children, the death of a friend or spouse, a person can feel the unrelenting jeopardy of life and erupt with fury against this faceless menace. This entails anger against God, family, business associates, even the dead who died without one's permission. It also involves a sharpened fear of one's own death and a persistent depression. The only solution, amid this mourning, lies in trusting the very people against whom one is furious and in reviewing the previous storms which one has survived. To take on, with new fervor, the ideals of the dead friends and to confront realistically one's own death is to gain a perspective in which first things come first. This becomes the heart of wisdom.

8. "One has to be mean to survive in this tough world": is the slogan for heightened competitiveness, intolerance, and self-preservation at any cost. It encourages a rabid buildup of isolating defense-mechanisms in one's work, unfounded fear of others, and protection of one's own weaknesses from

the gaze of close friends, even the spouse. One learns to despair of the young, the nation, the world, and the church and to speak of them with acid criticism. This self-absorption becomes as insufferable as a clammy, cold, prison cell.

If one fortunately discovers that there is no future in this depressing rediscovery of all the sins of the past, then with courage one can begin to feel a new protective gentleness toward the young, the family, new business associates, the poor and outcast, the struggling people everywhere. Out of this new tolerance can come a recovered sense of one's own individuality and rich talents. New hope in others breeds new hope in oneself and opens out into a reconciling wisdom.

9. "Where is God in all of this?": is the cry of the wounded, despairing person who feels that she is pitted against the whole threatening world in her loneliness. She can welter in waves of self-pity or can search for the Other, the great friend. There is no denying that each of the nine situations above can be alienating or reconciling, can end in hatred or love of self, can induce solidarity with others or isolation from them. They are really nine cries for God to enter into one's life and to give it a center of meaning and hope. He is wisdom itself and can turn the anguish of these nine crises into the satisfaction of moving toward wisdom and himself. To this end, the prayer of wisdom can be helpful. But what is this "lofty" prayer of wisdom?

3. Prayer of Wisdom for Embracing God and His World

Prayer of wisdom is an essentially contemplative prayer which enables one to peer deeply into the current event and at the same time to survey its total context. It is a marvelous prayer because it at once enables us to concentrate on the minute beauty of an incident and yet be aware of its cosmic significance. Naturally such prayer has stages of development through a person's life. If these stages are not distinguished and their different meanings are lumped under the one word "contemplation," this can be confusing to people. Indeed, it can halt growth by inducing false guilt about changing from one type of contemplation to another.

The first stage of contemplation is the *imaginative-sensuous* which is typical of the first and second weeks of the Ignatian Spiritual Exercises. Here one meets the Ignatian contemplations of creation and sin (perhaps done by way of prayer of reminiscence), the kingdom, the two standards, the incarnation, and episodes of Christ's life (perhaps done by way of prayer of Christ's memories).[5] In this contemplation one uses all five senses with all the range of emotions to color and to dynamize the images of the imagination so that their meaning becomes powerful in one's life.

The second stage of contemplation is the *aural-insightful* such as happens, for example, in the prayer of wondering[6] or in the prayer of listening where hearing and understanding are focused upon ongoing life around us and within us.[7] In the first prayer one looks quietly and long at events transpiring around one and wonders at their meaning for self, others and God without any attempt at categorizing them neatly for mental storage. In the second prayer one walks through the city or countryside questioning God: "Where are you, Lord?" Or one goes successively to Christ, Father, Spirit and Mary with the simple question: "How do you see me?"—and later returns to them, one by one, saying: "And this is how I see you."

In the third stage of contemplation, *radical prayer*,[8] one is living at the center of one's being. Prayer of centering takes us down there where the simple naming of Christ or Father or Spirit or Mary carries within it all the experiences of the first two stages of contemplation. It is as though all one's remembered experiences with the named person form a great net, and to pull one net-node (e.g. by using the name of Christ or by recalling a single Christ-event) is to draw in its train all these experiences to oneself. Only the name is needed since, like the name of the human beloved, it carries implicitly within it in a single moment every shared event.

Each naming, too, is a cry for deeper union with the one named—a union beyond all previous ones and typical of the third week of the Ignation Spiritual Exercises. Here the profoundest desires reach out for God as the central node and at the same time stretch out to others as the great web of God's people. This becomes the simultaneous living of the two great commandments.

Contemplation-in-action is the fourth stage.[9] It is the product of radical prayer and typical of the fourth week of the Ignatian Spiritual Exercises. Contemplation-in-action occurs when one focuses on a particular action (e.g. removing a brain tumor, selling bonds to a customer, watching a sporting event, cleaning house, gardening, repairing a faucet) and yet one is simultaneously aware of the whole surrounding context. This context happens to be the rich discoveries of the previous three stages of contemplation. Because of this, the contemplator-in-action is filled with confidence in his action, is sensitive to the presence of the Trinity in his work, and is guided by a joyful hope in the future results of his action. For this reason, the contemplator's actions are stronger, more persevering, more competent, and more free from anxiety about limitations or possible defeat.

Not so strangely, all four stages are equally needed to mutually enrich each other. For example, prayer of reminiscence keeps the contemplator-in-action aware of her personal history of defeats and successes, of strengths and weaknesses, of dependence on and independence of her community. Meanwhile prayer of Christ's memories keeps the contemplator-in-action aware that the episodes of Christ's life are pulsing within her own life events to companion her when she is trying to live Christian values within a pagan culture. At the same time, prayer of listening and prayer of wondering keep the contemplator-in-action attentive to the guidance of God and of Mary, while the prayer of centering, along with radical prayer, enables the contemplator-in-action to focus more strongly on the action being done rather than to be distracted from it. Reciprocally, the fourth stage, contemplation-in-action, furnishes sharper images for the first and second stages and stronger desires for the third stage of contemplation.

Of course these four stages of contemplation, being a wisdom process, are rooted in self-knowledge. The latter is needed to begin the healing of alienation from one's body and spirit. Only the down-to-earth wisdom of searingly honest self-knowledge can help a person recover self-respect. Such self-knowledge starts in the awkward adolescent search for values (Will I ever get it all together? Will anyone ever respect or love me?). Then it moves into the sometimes insufferable idealism of the young adult who may be tempted occasionally by an arrogant pseudo-wisdom to categorize older adults as crude, gluttonous, money-mad, selfish, manipulative, and hopeless.

Next comes the midlife discouragement-period with its experiences of personal limitations which can occasion negative reactions ranging from mild disappointment to fierce alienation and self-hate. At this time one begins to note with God's grace that the so-called "pure motives" of noble thought are often followed by seriously flawed actions, that the mean and the sordid lurk under one's nobility, and that subtle hypocrisy is never far away. At last, wisdom starts to rise when it finally dawns on this person that ugly motives were always there in her life. And so, despair of self can be right around the corner unless she gives thanks to God for his gifts and good motives, unless she recognizes that she cannot rip out her defects without ripping out at the same time her talents and goodness, unless she learns to live within her limitations, and unless she admits that God loves her as a total person, virtues and vices, gifts and quirks.

Behold: a new self-respect is born in her, not as a great doer, not as the perfect person having it all together, not as one supremely gifted in science or sports or business acumen, but simply as one to whom people and God have given unsolicited love. Out of this rugged humility the four-stage wisdom process can rise to teach her healthy self-love as the source for loving others and God.

But how does this wisdom process develop wisdom prayer for restoring self-respect? The response becomes clearer if one notes that there are two sides to the full contemplation-in-action which is this wisdom prayer: (1) finding God in each thing and event (analytic contemplation) and (2) contextualizing all things and events in God's presence i.e., finding all things in God (synthetic contemplation).[10] For example, the more analytic contemplation of Christ's life would concentrate on single gospel episodes especially where the interpersonal relations of *what* people say and do reveal the power of God at work in Jesus. In other words, the more analytic contemplation-in-action, as one would expect, will center more on individual events and persons for each one's unique meaning.

On the other hand, the more synthetic contemplation gathers the multiple insights from analytic contemplation into closer unity as one sees Christ's courage or honesty or kindness summing up numerous episodes into the *who* of Christ. So, too, the more synthetic contemplation-in-action is concerned with the context of events and personal relationships. It looks to the overall presence of God in many events and persons. Thus out of the person's contemplative wisdom (the analytic and the synthetic taken together) can issue wise actions. The latter carry within them simultaneously not only the awareness of individual persons, unique events, and the personal indwelling presence of Christ but also the awareness of the social presence of God and of his people in the world-context. This is wisdom prayer.

There is a second way of looking at the analytic and synthetic moments of contemplation-in-action as they constitute the prayer of wisdom. Finding God in all things, the analytic side of this wisdom prayer, enables the objective discovery of Christ present in the events outside me to stimulate me to become more aware of Christ within me (the subjective) and of the Trinity indwelling in me and others ("You have formed my inmost being; you knit me in my mother's womb. . . . Your eyes have seen my actions. . . . Were I to recount them [your designs], they would outnumber the sands; did I reach the end of them, I should still be with you" [Ps 139:13–18]). As a result, the contemplator-in-action, overwhelmed by Christ's omnipresence, allows the Lord to flush out of her mind-heart-actions all the overly clever conceptions, false ambitions, and petty schemes which would demean this presence.[11]

As a result, she feels somewhat confused and powerless precisely when God is most present within her felt emptiness and is most ready to strengthen her actions. Teilhard de Chardin shows the cause for her feeling of confusion: "The great mystery of Christianity is not that God appears (epiphany) but that God shines through (diaphany) the universe."[12] On the other hand, Dom Hubert Van Zellar echoes her sense of powerlessness in contemplation-in-action: "We look for Christ in darkness and in darkness He reveals Himself. We flounder in unsatisfied longing, and in our floundering we discover love. We think we have lost faith and hope, when in our seeming faithlessness and hopelessness we discover true faith and hope."[13] This is the paradoxical way in which prayer of wisdom makes us more present to self, God, and others. Thus the more subjective side of wisdom prayer is stimulated by its more objective side in analytic contemplation-in-action.

In contrast, the other more synthetic side of contemplation-in-action offers a reverse stimulation. When the contemplator-in-action experiences Christ's expansive presence invigorating, without exception, all events and persons not only of the contemporaneous present but also of the cumulative past, she is meeting the Lord of history. Her wisdom prayer is contextualizing all things in God. But this synthetic sweep of all events toward the omega point of Christ triumphant in his second coming (the objective side of wisdom prayer) does not happen unless the contemplator-in-action is first aware of the Lord of history within her as her constant companion (the subjective side). For without this inner conviction, the Lord of history can be merely a fanciful projection, not an objective reality pulsing the world. Thus on this synthetic side of contemplation-in-action, the subjective element of wisdom prayer stimulates the objective, not vice versa as in analytic contemplation-in-action.

These two sides of contemplation-in-action, the analytical (finding God in each thing and event) and the synthetical (contextualizing of all things in God), enable the contemplator-in-action to experience both wisdom and Wisdom itself. For such contemplation-in-action is the wisdom prayer which unites us with God and with his world by way of deeper self-knowledge, more awareness of others, and greater sense of God's immediate, yet obscure, presence. Thus do we regain our own self-respect, feel our personal dignity and achieve a new reconciliation with God and with the people around us. The self-hate or self-alienation slowly dissipates. We then know the warm gratitude felt by the demoniac for Christ's healing presence.

Chapter Four
The Deepest Wound:
Giving Up on Oneself

Honest self-knowledge eventually uncovers my basic defect such as subtle vanity, corroding jealousy, bitter vengefulness, lazy sensuality, or suspicious distrust of everyone. This destructive flaw may be revealed in a dramatic moment where I fail someone badly. Or it may appear in a midnight insight where I see my whole life riddled with the effects of this basic defect which at the moment seems to define me better than all my gifts and lifetime successes. I can become hypnotized by this negative root of all my sins and can wonder whether there is any hope for a person like me.

What is especially disheartening for me is the discovery that the basic defect is the other side of my basic strength. Like a tapestry, my personality has two sides to it, one beautiful-splendid and the other ugly-ratty. Thus the highly organized, efficient administrator may also be hard-nosed, overriding, and intolerant of slower people working under him. The good-humored, easy-going mechanic may also be remarkably lazy. The artist with a deep feel for beauty can be sensual and self-indulgent toward herself. The clever, inventive lawyer can be critical and impatient with his fellow lawyers' folly or clumsiness. The witty, comical saleswoman can be bitterly satirical and caustic with her clientele. The highly intelligent, foresightful city-planner may be overly cautious and even timid in making decisions. The shrewd, ever-provident grocer may be suspicious and distrustful of almost everyone.

The problem in dealing with this basic defect is that both sides of the personality-tapestry are woven out of the same threads. To do violence to the ratty side is to risk tearing apart the beautiful side since the basic defect is always inextricably woven within one's basic strengths. Here delicacy in living with the basic defect without letting it dominate one's decisions is the prescription. An overview of both these sides of self-knowledge is needed. For if only the dark side is considered, one risks undergoing a profound depression. On the other hand, if only the bright side is given credence, then blindness to one's faults can result in unreal estimates of one's gifts and opportunities. This can promote both arrogance and disastrous decisions.

1. Positive Benefits from Even the Dark Side

One benefit of finally discovering my basic defect can be that I accept myself for what I factually am without "delusions of grandeur." This enables me to stop dodging myself with the distractions of overeating, heavy drinking, drug taking, overwork, butting into others' affairs and so on. The alcoholic's cure is primarily based on recognizing his dependency and then boldly explaining it to others as partially due to his pride or selfishness or sensuality. Secondly, this recognition and admission, in turn, leads a person to be more compassionate (patiently and knowingly loving) with others in their struggles with a basic defect. A lawyer recently divorced for his extreme moodiness knows, as few others, the pangs of a client contemplating divorce and feeling that his ungovernable temper had brought him to the law office.

A third result may be a new reverence for oneself as a creature flawed but nevertheless loved devotedly by God and by others. Here gratefulness can rise toward God and these others for their patient love because only these lovers can compensate for one's basic defect and release one from its imprisoning atmosphere of lovelessness. For, after all, as Henri Nouwen notes: "Conversion is the discovery of the possibility of love."[1] When Israel complains to Yahweh: "You have hidden your face from us and have delivered us up to our guilt" (Is 64:6), the Lord replies: "I was ready to respond to those who asked me not, to be found by those who sought me not. I said: 'Here I am! Here I am!' to a nation that did not call upon my name. I have stretched out my hands all the day" (Is 65:1–2). Here the

patient love of Yahweh is ready and yearning to cover one's
defect and to strengthen the flawed person beyond his or her
expectations. But we tend to be fascinated by what is missing
rather than by what is present, just as the amateur art student
notes mainly the missing arms of the Venus de Milo and over-
looks the graceful contours of the body. We find it hard to
believe that the Great Artist is much more interested in our
gifts than in our flaws.

If one doubts all this, recall that God has created each of
us with a unique and mysterious defect which the flawed person can alone know through and through. The basic flaw is precisely one's creaturehood, the fact that one is not God. It is
unavoidable if one has come into existence as something less
than God, something not divinely perfect. For this reason it is
tightly woven within all one's gifts and positive qualities. Further, it embraces us closely until death. The vain peacock will
be brushing the dandruff off his shoulders, checking the part in
his hair, and smoothing his mustache as he topples with the
most charming grace into the grave. So, any desperate attempts
to eradicate one's basic defect can only weaken one's strengths.
The ascetic attempting to rid himself entirely of sexual temptations by stringent fasting may find the temptations more
appealing as his body weakens and clamors for a bit of pleasure
to restore its balance.[2]

It is well to recall also that it takes a while for a person to
discover his basic defect, so hidden is it in the mystery of the
self. Meanwhile God patiently loves us while he waits for us to
find it. One priest I know had more than a sneaking suspicion
that he was a coward, that his sensuality would not let him take
the chance of getting hurt; it was better to let someone else get
hurt. Then during his tertianship, a year of prayer and reflection on his past life of thirty-three years, he came to admit his
cowardice openly, an excruciating experience. So he began,
under direction, to try to live better with it. This meant that he
did not allow his defect to haunt him but accepted it more fully
as that which renders him more sensitive to others. In addition,
he needed to compensate for it by taking on some jobs where

he knew he could be badly hurt and by letting God into his basic defect: "When I am powerless, it is then that I am strong" (2 Cor 12:10).

He next discovered a strange fact: God was most intimate, most palpable, to him precisely in his cowardice. On one occasion, he had to confront a group of his fellow priests. He stewed for two months over the composition of a letter detailing his opposition to their earlier collective decision. With no small trepidation he went to the meeting called for by his letter. There, most of the group, boiling with anger, made it clear that he was like a domineering mother always talking freedom, but trying to squash it whenever the "children" took him at his word. Where ordinarily the priest would have cringed and felt beaten, this time he experienced unexpected strength and serenity. It was palpably evident to him that he was living on strength borrowed from Christ. His basic defect of cowardice was the place where Christ was most perceptibly present to him.

Sometimes this intimately felt presence of God within the basic defect is a sense of restlessness or unsettledness. A person's self-righteous complacency with herself may be disrupted by a sharp discontent with things as they are. It is so sharply felt because of its contrast with her usual self-satisfied laziness. This is how the call to a new strenuous apostolate or to an inconveniencing act of kindness may sound in the lazy person. It is the striking presence of God within her fatal flaw. Perhaps this can become clearer by studying two gospel personages who enjoyed dramatic basic defects.

2. Peter and Judas Face Their Destructive Flaws

Judas was beloved by Christ. Why else choose him as an intimate companion? He was sophisticated, organized, and careful. So it was quite natural to appoint him to hold the group's slim sum of money and to buy food, clothing, and lodging with shrewdness. When the apostles were sent out, two by two, to preach to the surrounding towns, Judas proved to be reliable and a good counterbalance for the fiery Simon of the

Zealot party (Mt 10:4). But somewhere along the line, Judas began to help himself to the money for his own conveniences. So when Mary anointed Jesus at the Bethany banquet, Judas protested: "Why was not this perfume sold? It could have brought three hundred silver pieces, and the money could have been given to the poor" (Jn 12:1–7).

Immediately after this "Judas went off to the high priests to hand Jesus over to them" (Mk 14:10), perhaps thinking that arrest by the high priests would force Jesus to declare himself the messiah and to enter into his kingdom where Judas would be one of the rulers. Incidentally, too, he would have money to tide him over during this period of transition. After all, did he not have the right to assure his future since he had sacrificed so much to follow Jesus? The betrayal was an ugly but necessary step in building the kingdom of the Father. Alienation from Jesus would be healthy and only temporary. So he thought.

Unfortunately events took a bad turn. At the last supper Jesus said, "One of you is about to betray me," and the apostles one by one questioned, "It is not I, Lord?" When Judas had to ask the same question, Jesus replied, "It is you who have said it" (Mt 26:20–25). Then Jesus dipped a piece of bread into a sauce and offered it to Judas as a last symbol of friendship. Judas accepted it "and immediately after, Satan entered his heart. Jesus addressed himself to him, 'Be quick about what you are to do'" (Jn 13:26–27).

Judas went into the night and alerted the authorities. They decided to trap Jesus in the garden of Gethsemane. There Judas "approached Jesus to embrace him. Jesus said to him, 'Judas would you betray the Son of Man with a kiss?'" (Lk 22:47–48). "Friend, do what you are here for!" (Mt 26:50). Judas felt his heart sink within him, but he continued to hold Jesus in his embrace until the temple police had bound Jesus' hands behind him. Judas, witnessing Jesus' swift condemnation and unexpected acceptance of death, "began to regret his action deeply. He took the thirty pieces of silver back to the chief priests and elders and said, 'I did wrong to deliver up an innocent man. . . .' So Judas flung the money into the temple and left. He went off and hanged himself" (Mt 27:3–5).

Judas' basic defect was likely his ambition and covetousness; he had to win, and at any cost to others. It was the other side of his gifts of intelligent providence and shrewd independence. Judas did not know himself very well and so probably did not suspect how vicious he could be. But his fatal flaw of covetous ambition had hardened him against compassion for Jesus and for the other apostles. As a result, he gave up on himself because he had first given up on Jesus' compassion for him. Our deepest fear ("Will I be any different from Judas?") makes him perennially fascinating for us. Earlier in our lives we were confident like Peter that we would never follow the path of a Judas. Later, after a few experiences of our own calculating betrayals, we wonder how sure we can be of our so-called integrity.

Peter's path was not greatly different from Judas'—except at the very end. It was the cocksure, impulsive ambition of Peter that led to his alienation from Christ. It took Peter a long time to admit that Christ was not deeply dependent on Peter's sure-fire advice, but that the opposite was the case. Only after the resurrection did Peter hear clearly: "As a young man you fastened your belt and went about as you pleased; but when you are older you will stretch out your hands, and another will tie you fast and carry you off against your will" (Jn 21:18). The evangelist Mark puts in stark contrast the warm generosity of Peter responding to Christ's question about his identity ("You are the messiah") and the impulsive presumption of his suggesting a change in the Father's plan for the messiah. To this Jesus must reply: "Get out of my sight, you Satan! You are not judging by God's standards but by man's" (Mk 8:29–33).

Even during the last supper, Jesus must remind Peter: "Remember that Satan has asked for you, to sift you all like wheat. But I have prayed for you that your faith may never fail." Peter, however, feels quite secure in his impulsive desire to please: "Lord, at your side I am prepared to face imprisonment and death itself." And so Jesus must tell him: "Peter, the cock will not crow today until you have three times denied that you know me" (Lk 22:31–34). After the resurrection, Christ's counter gift to the chastened Peter on the shore of Lake Tiberias is to allow him to express his love three times in answer to

Christ's challenging: "Simon, son of John, do you love me?" (Jn 21:15–17). The cocksure desire to please needed the balance of a more humble love.

Yet this was no sudden cure of Peter's impulsive desire to please. For Paul later had to confront him about his living two lives, one free from the law when working with the Gentiles and another under the law when meeting with the strict Jewish converts (Gal 2:11–14). Unlike Paul he did not relish being powerless; and so he impulsively compromised in order not to displease anyone. On the other side of this basic flaw, however, was his remarkably generous loyalty. Both flaws and strengths make him lovable to us—and to God. He seems so much like one of us. Consequently, the great difference in the lives of Judas and Peter was due not so much to their flaws and strengths but rather to Peter's refusal to give up on himself. Unlike Judas, he trusted in Christ's faithful love for him no matter how defective he might be.

A friend's story illustrates this trust. He told me that he had awakened with a midnight insight showing him the vicious effects of his vanity through fifty years of life. It was horrifying. But he said to the Lord, "I've stayed awake often enough with such insights to know that you want me to go back to sleep and to work this out with you in the morning." So he trustingly went back to asleep.

The next morning, as he was praying over this lifelong vanity, he recalled the time he was taking his elderly mother shopping and had said to her: "Mom, you never worry, do you?" She answered: "Not since the year you were graduating from doctoral studies. One evening during that year, your father and I were having a supper of biscuits and cocoa; it was all we had in the house and you never suspected this. I looked at a picture of Jesus in our kitchen and said to him: 'From now on, *you're* going to do all the worrying; I refuse to worry anymore.' And I haven't." My friend told me that he followed his mother's lead and said to the Lord: "I've been trying to deal with this vanity-streak in me for fifty years without much success; so from now on, Lord, I hand it all over to you and I refuse to worry about it any longer. I trust in your love for me." Could this be the trust needed to live with one's basic defect? But how is this confidence generated in a person? By some prayer of the community? Certainly not by merely solo prayer.

3. Prayer of Community: Source of Trust in Christ's Love

Let this statement stand before us to be challenged: despite the alienations of everyday living, WE ARE ONLY AS ALONE AS WE WANT TO BE. This must sound like the usual pollyanna palaver issued by those who have never felt chilling aloneness over a long period of time or who have never experienced abandonment by all those whom one valued. And yet could it be that "prayer of community" would make this statement relatively true? Here are some reasons why it may well be true that we are only as alone as we want to be.

First of all, Christ identifies, unites, or reconciles with the sinner before he sins, while he is sinning, and after he sins whether or not the sinner knows this or even cares about it. Unlike us, God is simply faithful without attaching any conditions such as "if you never sin again, if you have previously been a saint, if you pay your parish dues, if you give up satisfying food, if you love me more, and so on." He does leave the ninety-nine sheep and, when he finds the lost one, says to his friends: "'Rejoice with me because I have found my lost sheep.' I tell you, there will likewise be more joy in heaven over one repentant sinner than over ninety-nine righteous people who have no need to repent" (Lk 15:6–7). *More* joy in heaven— strong words. Should this not help us to see that Christ is on the side of us sinners, rather than on the side of those who think they have all the answers, all the virtues, for a holy life?

Matthew's (Levi's) big party celebrating Christ's call to discipleship dramatizes where the Lord's sympathies are. "While Jesus was reclining to eat in Levi's house, many tax collectors and those known as sinners joined him. . . . [The scribes] complained to his disciples, 'Why does he eat with such as these?' Overhearing the remark, Jesus said to them, 'People who are healthy do not need a doctor; sick people do. I have come to call sinners, not the self-righteous'" (Mk 2:15–17). Is it possible, then, to believe that we sinners are Christ's first interest?

If we were to believe this, would it not make some difference in our lives?

There is a second reason for saying that we are only as alone as we want to be: the Christian church is a church of sinners; we are all marginal people. When Christ says: "As often as you did it for one of my least brothers, you did it for me" (Mt 25:40), he happens to be looking at us, the hungry, the thirsty, the strangers, the naked, the ill, and the imprisoned. In other words, Christ surrounds us sinners not only with people who feed, welcome, heal, and free us, but also with himself present in each of these persons helping us. This is the church of Christ ministering to us, embracing us. I do not have to be pretty or to "have it all together" for him to have affection for me and for him to send his friends to take care of me. When I lived in a small Indiana town, the madam of the local house of prostitution was dying and she asked for the sacraments. To the scandal of many of her former patrons, she was buried from our little church fittingly called Our Lady of the Springs. How proud we sinners felt of our church. She is the church of the alienated, the lonely, the misfits, the anawim. We are at home in her and never quite alone. No matter what we do and no matter how terrible and persistent is our basic defect, we are first and always Christ's beloveds.[3]

The fact that Christ suffers in and with each of us during every alienation is a third reason for declaring that we are only as alone as we want to be. The proof of this? Consider how well Jesus identifies with Mary Magdalene when the apostles are irritated at her seemingly extravagant gesture of pouring the expensive nard over his body: "Why do you criticize her? She had done me a kindness. . . . By perfuming my body she is anticipating its preparation for burial. I assure you, wherever the good news is proclaimed throughout the world, what she has done will be told in her memory" (Mk 14:6–9).

How easily he identifies with the woman caught in the act of adultery who was dragged before him to be stoned to death. After the stoners had drifted away, one by one, cowed by his presence and by his writings in the sand, he says to her now alone: "Has no one condemned you? . . . Nor do I condemn you. You may go. But from now on, avoid this sin" (Jn 8:10–11). At once he protects her tenderly and then challenges her to leave the life of prostitution (which is perhaps the only life she has known) and to become what she has always wanted to be: a woman of dignity. Could he make this incredible challenge without the implicit promise to be with her and to be strengthening her all the days of her future life—precisely where she is weakest? In this way, Christ suffers in us so that we are never alone in our sometime misery.

The last reason for saying that we are only as alone as we want to be is Christ's gift of the sacraments. Their whole reason for existence is to heal alienations through the increased presence of Christ and of his people at key moments in our lives. Baptism is meant to birth us into the warmth of God's family from the outside cold of secular living. Then confirmation provides the courage to risk cultural alienation in order to protect and strengthen this family life of the church. Meanwhile the eucharist is reconciliation itself, a union with Christ and his people achieved through Christ's pouring his life-blood into each and all of us as he accompanies us throughout our daily chores. The sacrament of healing the sick enables Christians to regain the health needed to serve others and eventually to be enfolded at death into the communion of saints, the great community of the great today and tomorrow. Matrimony builds Christ's family in union with the witnessing church, one's supportive friends in faith. On the other hand, the sacrament of orders is meant to unite the priest with Christ in such a way that his preaching, offering of the eucharist, hearing of sins, marrying, baptizing, healing of the sick and serving of God's needy make Christ perceptibly present in this building of his family.

The sacraments, then, are offered to lift us out of the loneliness of our destructive flaw so that we can live strongly and creatively for God's family. They are the "prayer of community" surging through us every day in work, leisure, suffering, and joy so that Christ is truly Emmanuel (God-with-us). Indeed, his grace is the press of his presence in our bodies, minds and hearts. To accept the sacraments, then, is to accept Christ's trust in each of us and to respond by trusting him back. This mutual trust is the basic reconciliation which enables us to escape lonely alienation. For the "prayer of community" consists in the church forgiving each of us through Christ when we seem unable to forgive ourselves and to escape final alienation. This is why confession, the sacrament of reconciliation, is pivotal to our daily round of duties. It is life-saving.

4. Confession as Reconciliation with Self and Community

Today we are witnessing one of the great ironies of history. The sacrament of reconciliation (confession) is falling into disuse in the western church at the very time when it is most needed to restore the fragmented self and to unite conflicting groups with the church. Confession is the "prayer of community" struggling to heal the very roots of our being, namely our splendid gifts and our basic defect. What could be the reason, then, for lack of interest in this sacrament? Could it be that the sacrament of reconciliation has become for us routinized, dry, hardly hopeful, and seemingly a waste of our and God's time? If this be the case, is there any way by which we can change this experiential attitude?

One suggestion might be to use St. Augustine of Hippo's *Confessions* as a model for enjoying (yes, enjoying) the sacrament of reconciliation. When Augustine wrote *The Confessions* at forty-three years of age, he was a confused young bishop. The "snakes" within him—envy, lust, laziness, careerism— were writhing around just as they had been before his conversion eleven years earlier. If he compared his own conversion with the conversion stories of the idealistic Christian neoplatonism of his day, he had reason to wonder whether his conversion had been fake.

How could he continue as a bishop unless he reformed? So, he used a Freudian technique of writing his autobiography and a Christian custom of praying his discoveries with Christ. In this way, he slowly came to realize that God loved him totally, including both his basic defect and the past sins issuing out of his free connivance with this fatal flaw. It gave him sufficient hope to eventually become a saint and enough humility to keep him wondering why God was so good to him. Is it possible that

Augustine's experience could be ours? How would this occur concretely—especially in the sacrament of reconciliation previously so dry, boring, and fruitless?[4]

Within the "prayer of community" there are four steps which could perhaps lead me into God's welcoming affection amid my sins and basic defect:

1. I review what events have occurred in my life since my last confession or I survey any other period of time. I look only for the events which have given me (and the Lord) joy. The events can be big like a new friendship or middle-size like a vacation or small like good weather for golfing. But I gather them up and enjoy each of them again. In so doing, I discover how much I have to be grateful for. This joyful gratitude happens to be the first step toward Christian sorrow and hope.

2. I now note how, without even half-trying, my evil actions stand out clearly because of their sharp contrast against the good events. Due to their being historical events, both the good and bad are unique and fresh. No longer do I need to fall back on the drab, wrinkled grocery-list of sins which I once used over and over again like a tired elocution piece. In fact, I discover items I had never before noticed in my life. This is a bit disconcerting but it is certainly honest and not boring.[5]

3. To the priest I next confess first the good events—a bright surprise to him amid the darkness of sin-lists—by saying: "Father, God has been good to me these past weeks and I want to thank him here for. . . ." Then I move into the evil events and actions by saying: "Given how good the Lord has been to me, I'm ashamed and sorry for the following sins and tricks and selfish actions." Christian sorrow flows out of the triple sources: gratitude, admitted personal meanness and a graced sense of God's love for me.

4. The confessor now knows me better from the good events recounted and from the historically situated sins confessed. For confessing sins under generic headings yields little information. (Compare "I lied once" to "I lied to a long-

time friend about her doctor.") Because of the concrete details, the confessor can give more accurate and down-to-earth advice.[6] Then, too, he can suggest a more realistic penance than the cliché: "Say three Hail Mary's." If there has been much suffering in my life, he may say: "Spend five minutes making the stations of the cross, going from one station to the next and asking at each: 'How is it with you, Lord?' Then pause for six or seven seconds to give the Lord time to answer your question if he so wishes. If, as you move from station to station, the Lord begins to speak within one of these short pauses, stop and listen and forget the rest of the stations."

This four-step model enables me to experience my alienations from self, others and God without losing the hope and joy of being a Christian. For reconciliation is the other side of alienation. Christ is reuniting me at a new depth with himself, with the Father, with the seemingly disintegrating church-community, and with my own torn self. The mending and healing starts with me, but it ripples out from me to encircle my immediate family, then my neighborhood and parish, next my city and country, and finally my whole world.

Here is a rich form of "community prayer." Could its existence be the reason why we can survive our basic defects? Is this "prayer of community" the reason why we can go beyond survival to a recognition and acceptance of Christ's love for us even though we presently are steeped in sins, ashamed before self and others, and feeling wretched over our meanness? Is "prayer of community" the reason why we can discover new meaning in all the sacraments, but especially in that of reconciliation or confession? Is each of us, then, another Peter refusing to take the route of Judas? In other words, do we believe enough in Christ's love for us that we do not scale down his affection for us to the size of our own wrinkled hearts? Through "community prayer" do we hope enough in him to allow him to embrace us in warm welcome as did the father his prodigal son?

Chapter Five
Joseph of Nazareth's
Alienation from Mary[1]

PART I

One day I asked Joseph, the husband of Mary, some impertinent questions and got some pertinent answers.

Question: How did you come to know and to trust this
woman, Mary?

Joseph: I kept watching her. She was different. All the men
knew this and some of the women envied her for it. The young
men were a bit wary of her. I wasn't. She knew I was at ease
with her and it pleased her. Eventually I knew she liked me. I
had never thought of any other girl seriously—only of her
because I knew what was different in her. She had a prayerful
spirit, but also a playful one if you'll excuse the word. She was
serious, yet she had a deep joy in her which would bubble to
the surface—sometimes very unexpectedly—and this gave me
a sense of her trueness, her balance, her hope.

Then, too, I liked the way she did her work—sewing, cooking, working in the fields. She is steady, competent, dependable, seems to like her work but also enjoys the noonday break
and the funny things that sometimes happen to stop all work.
And she can stand up for a fair deal, too, when she's being
cheated of her full wages at the bazaar. She is the type of
woman who wears well—knows when to be quiet and when to
talk, is interested in people and will go out of her way for them
without much noise. So, there was nothing dramatic which
made me learn to trust Mary—just a lot of little days and jobs
and happenings which eventually showed me the inner spirit of
her life. She is a devout woman. God is real for her. She attends

synagogue prayers and prays alone in her house when she arises in the morning, when she takes meals, and so on.

Question: When did you realize your marriage was going to be different?

Joseph: At first when I was beginning to court her, I didn't know this. But gradually as I got to know Mary better, I sensed that her difference from the other girls was much greater than I had supposed. As we grew more familiar, she became more affectionate, more confiding, more trusting of me. Finally one evening she told me that she had made a vow of virginity to God and that God seemed to want her to continue this vow. I was puzzled and felt somewhat misled. But she explained that she had taken the vow at God's request and was never sure how long he wanted it to continue. She also said that God loved me, Joseph, and wanted her to be familiar with me because she would need me very much and I would be good for her. Both of us were mystified about what to do. I had not planned on vowing myself to virginity. What Jew ever did this? Even though Mary puzzled and intrigued me more than ever, I wondered seriously whether I should give up the thought of marrying her.

So I tried for a while to live without her. I went forty miles away to work and live with relatives. But life went dead for me; no other girl came close to interesting me—always I compared each with Mary and always I yearned to go back to her on any terms. Life was just desolate without her. So I returned to Nazareth and told her that I wanted to live with her to the end of my life no matter what had to be done. She was so glad to see me, so affectionate in her welcome, that I felt the separation was worthwhile just for this. I now knew the one thing I wanted in life—to make her happy, to protect her, to give her whatever she needed in life.

Question: What were your feelings about Mary's going to visit Elizabeth some weeks later?

Joseph: I knew I'd miss her, may have resented it, thought it somewhat impulsive of her (we had just been engaged). It all bothered me: the separation, the suddenness of her decision, the risk of the trip. I guess I was even angry and resentful at missing her again; three months were to seem like three years to me.

Question: When did you find out she was pregnant?

Joseph: After she got back from Elizabeth's place, one sabbath afternoon she took my hand and placed it on her stomach and said: "There is life here." I was shocked into a stupor. She then told me simply that she had not betrayed our vows. But I said to her: "This makes no sense to me." She looked deep into my eyes, touched my shaking hands and said: "I am mystified by all this, too. But please trust me and you will also be trusting God." I said: "Now what are you telling me—some new puzzle for me to live with?" She smiled and said: "Yes, the greatest mystery of all."

At that I got angry because she was serious and, again, I felt that my whole life was falling in ruins. I must have been suddenly shaking with sobs of frustration, fear, anger because I felt her take my head and put it to her shoulder and I felt her arms around me as though protecting me and trying to put me together where I had come apart like an old grain bag. I had not cried like this since my older brother died of fever—my closest friend, my constant companion. In fact, it was at his death fours years previously that I had discovered my deep need for God and human companionship and that I started to look for someone to share my life with. His death had led me to Mary and now she was holding me together literally.

After a while I wiped away my tears and told her that I had to get away to think. The look of torment in her eyes as I left her chilled my anger and got me almost to reach out to console her. But I didn't. I just walked away trying to make a little sense out of this night and my life. I cried out to the Lord on the dark path home but heard only my own voice. Death seemed almost pleasant compared to this bitter agony. I walked and walked and walked. Finally I turned home and slept like a dumb animal till the sunlight got so bright it awakened me to the terrible decision I would have to make.

Question: What was your decision then?

Joseph: I couldn't accept her explanation or, rather, her lack of explanation. I wondered if something had happened at Elizabeth's house during her three-month visit there. But then I also couldn't accept that she was unfaithful—not this woman. So, I prayed and prayed, waited and waited, and finally decided not to go through with the marriage but also not to let this be public. I would have some close friends in another village take care of both her and the child till I could find something better to do. My mind felt leaden and my heart crushed.

Question: Was this when you had the dream?

Joseph: Yes, after some weeks, just when I was going to take her to the distant village, I had this amazingly clear and strong dream in which I was told to take her as my wife and not to fear about contemning the law since she was still a virgin and had not done anything wrong but rather something wonderful. My dark thoughts lifted off but my wonderment simply increased. Who was I to act on a mere dream? Yet this dream was different—so clearly ringing of the truth. I at once told Mary. It was then I became aware of her impossible predicament. She had felt that she could not tell what had happened to her without breaking secrecy with God. Meanwhile, her anguish had been at least the equal of mine and she had tried to show me this with her affectionate words and touches. But in my confusion I had not been able to accept her affection because it might have weakened my decision to obey God's law about fornication. At this moment we hugged each other long. Both of us were laughing and crying at the same time. Then we started to wonder together what all this could mean as she now began to tell of Gabriel's coming, his predictions and the over-shadowing by God's spirit.

Question: Then what happened?

Joseph: The census of Quirinius directed us to Bethlehem and I believe you know the rest of the story.

❁　　　❁　　　❁

PART II

1. Questioning-Wondering Prayer

When someone is undergoing alienation, questioning prayer naturally arises in the heart—as it did with Mary. "Mary treasured all these things and reflected on them in her heart" (Lk 1:29; 2:19, 33, 51). This prayer also rose in Joseph, a stalwart patron for alienated lovers who want to give life but feel like death. Questioning prayer is a wondering which finds no easy answers to its questions. Yet it is not a distrusting or cynically doubting prayer about God and others. Instead, it is a fiercely honest prayer like that of Job or of Jeremiah's third lamentation. It is concerned often enough with why Yahweh lets good people suffer while evil people seem to prosper: "Why, Lord, do you stand aloof? . . . For the wicked man glories in his greed, and the covetous blasphemes, sets the Lord at nought. The wicked man boasts, 'He will not avenge it; there is no God.' . . . In hiding he murders the innocent; his eyes spy on the unfortunate" (Ps 10:1–8. Cf. also Ps 73).

The person questioning and wondering in prayer believes firmly that Jesus does not waste a moment's suffering but always draws good out of it eventually. But the long wait to see the good can at times stretch one's faith to the breaking point. I remember an elderly man describing with a wry smile how his high school acne made it an exquisite agony to meet on the street young ladies he knew. What was worse was going to a dance with his acne covered by facial powder. Once there and feeling like the son of Frankenstein, he would often enough be refused a dance and have to face the remarks of the "guys" when he returned from the refusal. He remembered one day saying within himself: "I'll never judge another person by externals again, Lord, with your help." But it was only decades later that he realized how influential that perduring decision had later been for him in his job as a personnel director for a trucking firm. The long wait between the question ("Why do you let this happen to me, Lord?") and the provisional answer ("Because, my friend, . . .") enables wondering prayer to open out into the prayer of trust during the long alienation period.

For these reasons, Joseph, the man of questioning-wondering prayer, is a good patron of family life where the wait between a deep question and a satisfactory answer is frequently not only long but also excruciating. A glance at Joseph's life hints at this conclusion. When Mary returned pregnant from her visit with Elizabeth and Zechariah, the center of Joseph's world, built with such care, crumpled without the slightest explanation. Later his relatives in Bethlehem turned out to be hardly hospitable to his obviously pregnant wife, and desperately he had to use a cave-barn for their shelter. Still later, during the Egyptian exile, the handyman Joseph must have striven hard to gather a clientele of customers even in the Jewish ghetto; there were no friends there to help him.

Nor was the return from exile much better as he moved out of the charming Jerusalem suburb of Bethlehem to the backwater town of Nazareth because of the continuing persecution of the Herod family. Finally, his early death, the overarching fear of any young husband, made it impossible for him to provide well for the future of his wife and foster son. All this made Joseph become an expert in alienation/reconciliation. No wonder he is the universal patron of those fearing final estrangement in death. To survive, he had to be as hopeful as Abraham, his fellow wanderer in exile; as compassionate as Joseph the patriarch to his uncompassionate relatives of Bethlehem and Nazareth; as faithful and sensitive as David to Yahweh's providential mercy; as convinced of God's goodness as Job in his many misfortunes; and as trusting as Jesus, his son, who had to leave so much of his work seemingly unfinished.

Unfortunately or fortunately, as one interprets the times, we of the late twentieth century have questioning-wondering prayer as our more characteristic way of responding to God.[2] Since when have there been so many wars, both hot and cold, on almost every continent? What other half-century has enjoyed a world-destroying threat of nuclear warfare? Since when have famines been so devastating and widespread that they are called self-perpetuating? Since when have the economically imperial countries so dominated the world that one group of nations (the so-called fourth world) has been abandoned as economically irredeemable? Under these conditions does any other type of prayer than the questioning-wondering variety make as much sense?

Questioning-wondering prayer, far from being an enervating doubting, is an entering into mystery. The mystery may be natural like love, friendship, commitment, fidelity, death, suffering, infant gestation and the atomic particle. Or it may be beyond the natural like Christ's incarnation, the Trinity's interpersonal life, human resurrection, Jesus' cross, his sacraments, and the church as Christ's body. To enter a mystery with a large group of people is an awesome experience, but to enter it alone is frightening. Yet the modern day Christian enters mystery without the societal support one had in the nineteenth century or in medieval times. As a result, cynical doubt, the sworn enemy of questioning-wondering prayer, can more easily insinuate itself to throttle this prayer. Mystics of the modern era like Simone Weil and Thérèse of Lisieux have specialized in questioning God and wondering at his providence; we are not so alone as we might have thought.

Besides, this questioning-wondering prayer is paradoxically nourished by the baffling discoveries of mysterious subatomic particles, by the stubborn evils discovered in the human psyche through the advances of psychology and psychiatry, by possible manipulation of the national mind through clever communication ploys, by genetic engineering feats, by the economic buccaneering which jeopardizes millions of families, by the contemporary relativism of values which makes us yearn for stable value-constellations for our guidance—to name only the more obvious problems. How do they nourish questioning-wondering prayer? They force us to question and wonder about the meaning of life. This is the point at which prayer begins its deepest fumbling for God's presence and its most acute listening for his word.[3] It is also the point where trust can arise out of life's mysteries even though the particular mystery of the moment seems but a great void.

2. The Paradox of Trust amid Questioning-Wondering Prayer

One might expect questioning-wondering prayer to reduce the level of trust in God and others. The opposite is the case. For the root of all our loves of God and others is trust, and the growth of this trust, paradoxically, depends on questioning these loves (without denying them) and on discovering with wonder their deep roots of trust. Let me tell four stories to illustrate what is meant here.

The first story indicates how trust is the root of love and how its destruction withers the deepest love. I had been working with a couple for ten years to help them save their marriage with its four children. During those years there had been several separations, some heart-rending events (the death of one child), and many spats accompanied by occasional physical violence. But always healings occurred and I began to feel some confidence that their marriage would perdure when they invested in a large new home. One morning, two years later, the husband appeared at the front door, wearing sunglasses to hide his bruises. After talking for two or three hours with him and later some hours with his bruised wife, it gradually dawned on me that all trust had drained away from their relationship. Divorce became inevitable even though they and their children were to suffer much from the incurable alienation. It was my turn to do the questioning-wondering prayer.

The second story illustrates how the prayerful questioning of a love can strengthen rather than weaken it. In working with a young man concerning his prayer life, it became clear to me that he found it very hard to trust anyone and that he also needed psychiatric counseling in the area of sexuality. With the help of the psychiatrist, he came to understand that these two matters were connected. As a child he had been sexually abused by an older boy whom he had at first idolized. Later he was falsely accused of insulting his mother and physically beaten for this by his much admired father. Two idols had been smashed. Could anyone be trusted—including himself? After ten years of therapy, fifteen years of spiritual direction and twenty years of prayerfully questioning his many relationships (he was by now a respected doctor happily married with three children), he could now begin to wonder at the beauty of his loves and to recognize how trust was finally rooting these loves. A deep alienation stretching back to early childhood had been finally healed by his prayerful questioning and wondering.

The third story shows how prayerful questioning issues into a wondering prayer. I had made eight annual retreats with a masterful spiritual director who at last said to me: "Do you realize that over the last thirty years you have made seven basic decisions, each changing your life significantly, and that you have fought each one of them, backing into them rather than facing them? You couldn't believe that God liked your decisions because you couldn't fully trust your advisors or yourself. When are you going to face-front into your basic decision of this retreat and to fully trust yourself, your advisors and your God?" Somehow I did face-front and make this eighth decision to give up tenure at my university, to ask for a research professorship, and to start completing the book-manuscripts hauntingly piled on top of the file cases in my room. But what gave me courage here was to see in my prayer how deeply, through the years, Christ, my fellow Jesuits, my students and my friends had trusted in me. I had not been wondering simply about my own self-trust but also about their trust in me.

The fourth story sketches out for me how trust can be found in the midst of a terrible alienation if one is willing to question and wonder prayerfully. One Lenten evening after I had offered the eucharist at a local parish church, a middle-aged couple gave a testimonial to God's trust in them and their trust in him. The wife spoke of how lucky she had felt to marry her young husband—a warm, protective, witty man. She had expected much companionship from him, but in their first years of marriage he was going to evening law school and working as a salesman. By the time he was practicing law they had three young boys.

Then he got into city politics and again his nights were filled with meetings while two more boys were born. She found herself needing a martini or two to solace her loneliness while cooking supper after the long day of corraling five high-spirited boys. The time came when she would ask herself: "I wonder who cooked the dinner we're eating." Then came the occasion when she slid under the dinner table in a stupor. Her husband quickly curtailed his political work to help her deal with the alcoholism. The alienation between them gradually healed as they prayerfully questioned their life and wondered about their future.

The five boys once again could feel safe—until precisely at this time her husband was afflicted with a spinal disability which stretched him prone on his bed for some months. There was plenty of time for them to do more questioning and wondering prayer. At last the doctor scheduled surgery for a Monday morning. On the preceding Friday morning, her husband was able to get out of bed without any help or pain and take breakfast in the kitchen. Previous to this, he had left the bed only, with excruciating pain, to be assisted to the bathroom. Hardly believing what was happening, the couple reported this to the doctor who had them come down to his office immediately for x-rays. The spinal lesion had disappeared. A final note: a year later they at last had a baby girl for whom the prayer of questioning-wondering is not totally responsible—though it does seem to have healed alienations for them by helping them to trust each other and God more deeply.

The prayer of questioning-wondering, then, uncovers the depths of our love where trust lies, enables that trust to grow, increases one's wonder at the beauty of love and trust, and begins the healing of long-time alienations. What would have happened to all us questioners and wonderers if Mary and Joseph had not prayerfully questioned and wondered about the events of their lives? What would have happened to each of us if we had successfully throttled this prayer in ourselves?

Chapter Six
The Loneliest Experience:
Mid-Life Divorce[1]

Helen's husband had confronted her a year ago after a very quiet dinner. "Helen," he had said, "there is something we have to talk about in the living room while the kids are out." They had sat there through a long silence before he said in a rush of words: "I want a divorce; I can't go on living as we have been—distant, on parallel courses, never really meeting. The kids already suspect something and are old enough to handle this now. I've made a decision and no talking will change it. I don't want to hurt you any more than I've already done. My lawyer has drawn up the legal papers; you'll be taken care of financially."

Helen, her voice sounding like cracking ice, had said to him: "Joe, it's Anita, isn't it? That day down at the office I saw the glance you gave her—like the one you had once given me." "Yes," he said, "but we are not going into that." Helen could recall herself slowly getting up, slowly going up the stairs to her room, throwing herself on the bed and beginning to shudder with great dry heaves. No tears, only a terrible emptiness.

When, during the course of the following weeks, she had been alone with each of the children, she had received some additional shocks. Jim, the twenty-two year old just finishing college, put it simply: "Look, Mom, where have you been the past two years? Dad has been home less and less, and telling less and less what he's been doing. What have you been thinking?" The twins, Edith and Carol, high school seniors, were rather casual: "Mom, this is the way things go these days; you have to be ready for the worst and this is the worst, no doubt about it." Timothy, the twelve year old, was unconsolable: "Dad's leaving us behind and it's unfair; I hate him now. But what can we do? I guess we just get used to it the way Jerry Kanz did when his Dad moved out."

Helen, like many another to-be-divorced woman, had looked back over her life and wondered bitterly: Where did it start to go wrong? Where did I fail? Except for Timmy, the children seemed so casual about it all. Were they simply ungrateful, without any affection for her and Joe, or were they covering up their anger and disappointment? Her telephone call to her mother had caused a flood of tears and a scalding anger—more at Helen's stupidity than at Joe's two-timing. Her favorite brother had only said, "Well, the bastard finally owned up to it, did he?" Women friends had been properly shocked and consoling for some weeks; then the telephone calls became less frequent and one friend finally said to her: "Honey, you have to stop lamenting and get your life together—without Joe; the sooner the better." All her doings had become meaningless: cooking meals, housecleaning, shopping, bridge-clubbing, fulfilling the immediate needs of her children, attending mass, telephoning friends, volunteering at the hospital, watching TV late into the night.

Then the depressing guilt-fits began. Why were her children so unfeeling unless she had failed badly in their upbringing? Why had she not noticed sooner her husband's wandering and done something to woo him back? Had she become an insensitive creature herself? Were all her friendships superficial, revealing her own lack of depth? Was all her busyness merely a way to hide from herself who she really was: an empty shell of a woman? How could even God find time for her anymore? Actually her past seemed gutted, her present confused and her future dark with anxiety.

1. The Woman Religious' Parallel Experience of "Divorce"

Helen's experience, in one form or another, is that of thousands of wives and mothers as divorces continue to multiply across America. But is it so very different from the experience of not a few women religious who at mid-life review the past ten or twenty years of their own lives and wonder where their prayer-union with Christ has gone?

The woman religious has been living the regular routines

of a life consecrated to Christ: spending some time with him before breakfast and before heading to bed; taking care of his people in hospital, school, daycare center, parish, and social work office; making some friends along the way; watching TV and going for occasional walks; attending family gatherings, and centering her life in daily eucharists.

But in everything she feels hardly any feed-back of gratitude or joy. If she is a social worker, she may have been called a meddler by the family whose children she has seen through hospitals, remedial reading courses, and angry bouts with their parents. The high school teacher of twenty-five years' experience may have been told by a lay colleague that she is twenty years behind the times in her teaching techniques and thirty years behind in her understanding of today's high schoolers. The sister-nurse may be overwhelmed with the ugly fact that her order's hospitals are now big business and that she had better play it safe with charity cases lest the hospital's budget-report show red ink. An almost exhausted sister may be informed by her superior that if she cannot take this job of religious coordinator at the disorganized St. Dismas parish, she had better find another job to earn her way. Meaning seems to have drained out of her work. The once beautiful routines connected with teaching, nursing, administrating, catechizing, parish organizing, and social working feel drab, spiritless, and unending.

Meanwhile, because of her busy dedication to her order and its works, she has allowed her own brothers and sisters to fade out of her life as they moved to the distant coasts and as she wrote less and less often. Her parents have become elderly, somewhat absentminded, eager for her presence but hardly able to carry on a relaxing conversation, and evoking melancholy in her at their decline and helplessness. Her sister-friends are as busy as she—glad to see her and to chat for a time, but always on the move to another appointment; little time for long leisurely conversations, not many fun times. Because she is one of the few younger sisters in her older community, she may have to assume greater responsibilities without any contemporary nearby in whom to confide and with whom to laugh at life's crazy antics. This is a new aloneness never felt in her initial formation. The simple joys of life seem few and far between during these periods of intensely felt alienation.

She wonders: Is all my past life for nothing? Have I lost the respect of my own family, those who first gave me life and hope? Have I missed out on community life? Or did it never exist and I pretended that it did? Why has my ministry lost its zest? Have I begun to give up on it and, if so, will I ever find a second ministry and trust myself to its demands for a disciplined life of sacrifice? Do my superiors and fellow religious value me for myself or only for what I can do? Are we all just worker bees in the religious hive? Where is the reality of my prayer life? God seems so distant, so uninterested in me, so unlike the intimate friend of my early religious life. Around me I seem to find so many happy families and fulfilled career women. Or am I just romanticizing their lives out of my own drabness?

Then begin the guilt-fits. How did my life dissipate into merely constant duties, deadlines, hurried moments of leisure with friends, community tensions, and superficial moments with Christ? How could I have let it happen? Does all this mean that I never had a vocation to religious life or that religious life in my particular group is now antiquated and no longer viable in our present culture? What is my future—if anything?

Who but a recently divorced laywoman could fully appreciate these questions and feelings of the woman religious? The divorced man, hearing a man religious voice similar questions and feelings, would surely resonate to these pains of the heart and mind.

2. The Feel of Alienation from the Church Among the Divorced and the Alienated

The suffering asked of divorced men and women and of alienated religious is scandalous not only to them but to the people who love them dearly. The shock felt by the "divorced" is such that at times they do feel isolated from their family (blood or religious) and perhaps even from Christ's church.

Their great temptation is to cut loose from past ties, to be free
from all the baggage of the past. They ask themselves: "Why
not just leave the family or the religious order and forget any
service of the church?" It seems so much easier simply to concentrate on a career and, if the occasion offers, to form a small
manageable group of new friends. Later some of these
"divorced" will leave the church deliberately and others will
slowly drift away complaining: "I'm tired of fighting church
bureaucracy and small-mindedness."

There is no denying that, in the twentieth century church,
scandals are frequent. The petty pride of place, the drift toward
disorder, the trickery practiced in the name of the kingdom,
the mechanical use of the sacraments, the eloquent extolling of
poverty by comfortable clerics, and the depreciation of wom-
en's ministry are all very much alive. In fact, Christ found them
quite active in his first century church: the women's announce-
ment that they had met the risen Christ was called "women's
gossip"; John and James used their mother to agitate for their
occupying the seats of power next to Christ; Paul had to confront Peter about using different standards for Jewish and Gentile converts; Jerusalem converts tried to saddle all Gentile converts with the heavy apparatus of Judaic law; Ananias and
Sapphira embezzled the common holdings of the Christian
community; some of the apostles, notably Judas, deplored Mary
Magdalene's ministry to Christ as frivolous. This is the kingdom, God's people, as Christ described them in the parables
where the net is thrown into the sea to haul in both good and
bad fish or where the wheat field is sown with weeds by the
enemy.

The problem is not that scandal is always in the church but
that faithfulness is needed to live through the scandalous events
amid feelings of alienation. Men and women religious suffering
alienation from their communities need to share their lives with
divorced laymen and laywomen if they are all to remain faithful
to the church and to their families, lay and religious. The pool-
ing of experience, the companioning in common sorrows, the
cooperative attempt to let the church know their agony, the

working together to build better futures for each other and for the church—all these enable the "divorced" to take heart and to remain loyal.

One woman religious who has been offering a program for divorced women in her motherhouse found that the prayers of the retired sisters gave solace to the divorced women, while the faith of the divorced women amid severe mental suffering proved encouraging to elderly sisters, some of whom felt intensely their seeming uselessness to the world and to their church. One of the divorced women approached this woman religious directing the program and said to her: "Were you divorced before you entered religious life? You seem to read us so well." Aloud the sister said: "No, I've never been married," but whispered inside herself "But I have experienced divorce—from my congregation."

Recently women and men religious groups have been welcoming some divorced into their communities and finding that these women and men bring in a dimension of life much needed by the religious order. The divorced woman or man has gone through devastating bereavement from all that once gave meaning to her or his life. Through this stripping, they have rediscovered their own personal worth, having learned how to distinguish life-roles (mother or father, wife or husband, secretary or carpenter, daughter or son, sister or brother) from their own selves which play out these roles.

The divorced woman, for example, no longer defines herself merely by what she can do, but by what she can be—first in herself and then for others. This, of course, affects her relationship with Christ. She is devoted to him, first of all, for his own sake, and she expects his affection to be directed toward her for herself and not simply for her accomplishments. Neither God nor she herself is made out to be an heroic workaholic. Such a mature attitude can be benevolently contagious.

On the other hand, women and men religious have something to offer divorced laywomen and laymen. After all many religious have had to deal with the midlife transition.[2] They have come to see that the "yesterdays outnumber the tomorrows" and that they have to trim their apostolic sails accordingly. Their energy is less, their talents are not quite as rich as they first thought, they must drop some projects totally, others partially, in order to do the central works. At this point envy of the younger, the more energetic, and the more talented can creep in. Amid these tensions, one becomes more aware of personal shortcomings, pretenses, sins of revenge and cattiness, and suddenly vehement sex-drives.

This discouraging aspect of life is often allied with a sense of being enmeshed in a great bureaucratic machine (at the job or in the congregation or in work with the local government) with which one must battle for personal values without destroying oneself or the organization. At this same time friendships take on greater importance and one must reorder one's commitments to people, work, and God. Here the "divorced" man or woman faces bereavement from parents and older friends who die. Meanwhile they have moved away from pet projects, from former work that gave much satisfaction, and from favorite attitudes or ideas that no longer fit the times. Death, including their own, seems at times to totally surround them.

But at the same time, if the "divorced" can ride all these waves with some gratitude and graciousness, the slower pace allows them to have time for more care of others. A warm wisdom, the fruit of keeping a sense of humor amid much suffering, can pervade their every day. A new stability may take shape at the center of their beings. In their lasting friendships, they may rediscover their faithful God. And all this they can offer to other "divorced" men and women out of the very alienations which they have felt toward their own families or congregations.

How bountiful the divorced lay people and alienated religious can be toward each other and toward other alienated people of God—even though at times they feel so utterly empty and find themselves walking laboriously as though in desert sands. This desert experience has been chronicled and deserves our attention since out of it can come a conversion which will reveal a new self, a new God and a new world. Could the experience of alienated religious carry insights needed by divorced laymen and laywomen?

3. The Desert Experience of Transition Before Conversion

Two women have given us brutally honest yet sensitive accounts of their transitions from one congregation to another. The great change seemed to them like a lay person's divorce and remarriage with its moments of awkwardness, periods of loneliness, and rediscovery of self and life.[3] Sr. Marie Conn found the loneliness of transfer to a new religious community unique in its roots and in its intensity. For she left behind a vibrantly rich past with only a vague future in mind. Besides, those with whom she would live her present and future had little idea of her past and she had equally little idea of their past. When one starts all over with new and slowly developing friendships, with fresh routines, and with no one able to enter into one's more precious memories, one is thrust into a new relationship with God where trust is paramount and where sensitivity to the outcast is sharpened.

Sr. Anne Steinacker describes her gradual alienation from her original congregation's new processes, plans, aims, and style of life—despite her love for the community. The resultant conflict caused anguish and instilled the fear of losing her religious vocation. Then came the thought that her religious vocation might be to another congregation. But she smothered this possibility only to find that the ensuing frustration and anger were driving her into deep depression. This double jeopardy demanded therapy and a long wait for clarification of mind and heart. Out of this issued a slow acceptance of her true identity as simply Anne. Because of seemingly chance happenings, she had to break with her own community and become reacquainted with the community of her youth through her ministry with them. The process of disenchantment had taken fifteen years, but her decision to join the second community restored peace which eventually became a strong happiness. Is this experience so different from that of divorced lay people who each have had to pick up the pieces of a former world and refashion them into the new world of the divorce situation?

What these women endured was the desert experience which results from alienation and which, if faced honestly, precedes conversion. This common experience of the divorced woman or man and of the alienated religious has at least six characteristics. First of all, at least temporarily, one's past and present seem meaningless because they do not seem to fit the future toward which the world of everyday life is moving at a fast pace. One's skills and interests do not appear marketable; and so, one has a sense of standing still within one's own emptiness. Further, the alienated person's horizon of values whereby he or she gets direction and finds roads for measuring progress seems to have disappeared. Third, this isolates a person from others, including the absent God, and one is tempted to escape loneliness by joining others in superficial relationships and in mind-deadening routines of overwork or bar-hopping or club-going or sports entertainment.

One's emotions are also frozen by the cool efficiency of the great bureaucracies of government, business, church, and education, so that one feels flat, ambitionless, yet quietly revolutionary. Fifth, the security of thinking that one knows one's future crumbles under the divorced person. The finances of the divorced lay people are reduced sharply because of supporting double households. In a similar way, many religious orders of women and some of men are in such dire financial straits that they cannot take care of their members much less those leaving their ranks. Lastly, time is running out and demanding a reevaluation of all one's relationships, skills, and meager hopes.

And yet thirst for God can remain even in this desert experience; it is the only oasis of security during the day's plodding through the shifting, thick sands of frustrations, duties, and disappointments. It is what led Dorothy Day through "the long loneliness" after her divorce. It is what led Teresa of Avila through Spain to reform the Carmelite convents—each a hornet's nest waiting to sting her—while she underwent the dark night of the soul. It is what led Thérèse of Lisieux to endure the pus-filled sheets in the laundry, her superior's neglect of her tuberculosis, and the consequent severe depression which made her deathbed seemingly into a divine divorce court. Perhaps it would prove worthwhile to consider the conversion process occurring within this desert experience so that the divorced people and alienated religious can take hope and perhaps rediscover their prayer life.

4. Conversion and the Prayer of Frustration-Peace

Amazingly, out of the frustrating alienations which one experiences in the divorce situation, there can rise a strong prayer of peace, a new way to see the whole world. This is the mark of an ongoing conversion. How does this happen? The divorced person or alienated religious finds herself or himself going far beyond previous experience to entrust the self entirely to God and to his people. Contrarily, on previous occasions he or she had tried to keep control of the situation by putting God on a shelf or by losing self in routine prayers and busyness so that God could be kept at bay. The new attitude is a liberation: "I own the whole world because I own myself and not merely my little dogmas, certitudes, and securities (home, food, comforts, bank account); I'm no longer afraid to depend totally on God and others."

This sense of totality, this feeling that the one God fills the universe and leads it persuasively toward a great destiny, unifies those dichotomies which previously had torn the divorced person apart: joy/sorrow, freedom/commitment, God/people, individual/community, and contemplation/action. The divorced person or alienated religious has let God into her or his life with utter simplicity. As a result, the Lord's affectionate presence can help the divorced and alienated to unify their lives with a total commitment to him. Such a commitment opens out inevitably toward expansive care of others with new hopes, motives, and even humane techniques. For the divorced or alienated person has left the confining apartment of self-pity to walk the great boulevards of the city of God.[4]

This conversion experience is, of course, a wisdom process inducing peace into one's life. But one progresses with some

pain toward the contemplative prayer called peace-out-of-frus-
trations through the following eight stages:

1. *Facing* the alienation directly after dodging it for some time.
   (Does anyone ever face the divorce-situation before using a
   dozen tricks to distract herself or himself from the truth?)
2. Taking *hope* that with the Lord's help this problem can be
   lived with even if it is never more than partially solved. (A
   huge step requiring a drastic realism which is often called
   humility. The romanticism of false hope is rejected for a
   true hope that stings.)
3. Gradually *making* some *sense* out of the divorce or alienating situation by sorting out its elements and discovering
   some small answers. (Counseling may help here; certainly
   consultation with friends and family members is necessary.
   Not to seek expert advice where needed is to cripple this
   wisdom process.)
4. Being confident that so long as I try to choose with intelligent honesty what is right and just, I will be doing *God's will*
   no matter what the outcome of the choice. (The honest trying is what counts with God, not the success or failure of my
   choice.)
5. Being attracted to one of the possible choices even though
   it may be the *hardest* to do. (This takes poised freedom—
   Ignatian indifference—which is the willingness to suffer
   harshly for what is better for me and for others. It is a refusal
   to take the easy way out simply because it is easier.)
6. Feeling *relief,* after much sweaty deliberation, at having
   reached a provisional decision. (Here peace is first felt rising
   out of previous frustration. The deliberation, before taking
   any action, is actually a contemplation of all the factors rel-
   evant to the situation of alienation and to its cure. Patience
   is the name of the game at this point.)
7. Being willing to *hold back* from this provisional decision if
   it should be found unfair to others. (Such thoughtfulness for
   others gives validity to the whole wisdom process since it
   insures that awareness of God suffuses the process—the

God who said "Whatever you do to the least of these my brothers you do to me.")

8. Setting the decision into *action* and watching it work out through the divorce situation. (Always there is need to keep reshaping this decision according to its consequences and to the changing elements of the situation. But the first seven steps carry within them the prayerful attitude which can make such reshaping prudent, just, courageous, and well-balanced.)

This contemplative prayer of frustration-peace (so named because both are co-present in the experience) will often be put under attack by those who envy the newly found peace of the alienated person: members of the family, one's own false guilt, one's enemies, and even Satan. The source of this attack on one's peace can be recognized as evil with these four criteria:

1. There is a *sudden* entrance of dark insight or fear to disturb one's peace in contrast to the Lord's gradually enlightening and instilling of conviction to give peace. In this abrupt intrusion there are no eight steps of wisdom but simply one piercing thrust into one's mind and feelings. (Once a retreatant, previously sailing along in peace and joy, came to me sweating and fear-ridden. In his consciousness he had heard his wife saying with stunning clarity: "Al, you are never wrong; you are the perfect boy scout." Suddenly he had seen into his condescending ways with his wife and six children through twenty-four years of marriage.)

2. The attack is based on a *vicious half-truth.* (Yes, Alfred has condescending ways. But he is also a loyal husband, a thoughtful father, a hard worker, a respected person and a generous man. The Lord's insight into self is always incisive and unforgettable, but never one-sided, never without a reassuring affection, never bitter, never hopeless. Unlike the attack with half-truths, it eventually gives peace and leads to wisdom.)

3. The *strategy* of the enemy is *simple:* aim at the peaceful person's basic weakness with a devastating brief formula or
   vivid memory with which one cannot argue because of its
   brevity and vividness. Then hint that this is the whole truth
   and the only truth. (The sound of his wife's voice in her brief
   encounter with Alfred rings clear in his consciousness. Then
   the enemy insinuates: "You are merely a boy scout; everyone knows this and scorns you behind your back: you are
   too old to change." Meanwhile the Lord encourages the
   embattled man to use some equivalent of the eight wisdom
   steps in dealing with this alienation between himself and his
   wife. This last is a growth process, not an attack.)
4. The attack is meant to undermine, *paralyze, even kill* if possible. (The enemy says: "Your type of Christianity is rotten
   like yourself. So, relax and enjoy what's left of the world and
   of your life. And if you can't do that, get drunk and drive
   into the Chicago River. That will give you the peace you're
   looking for." The Lord's message differs: "Like any Christian you have your sins and limitations. But this is your
   chance to grow in the midst of the alienating situation.
   Learn to live humbly, realistically, with your vanity; people
   still admire and love you for the many things you've done
   for them. Be at peace." Thus the Lord's strategy is directly
   counter to the enemy's. The Lord instills confidence, liber-
   ates and gives fuller life. In this way, the very attack itself
   can be the occasion for the rise of this prayer of frustration-
   peace. Cooperation with the Lord in not yielding to this
   attack becomes a strengthening of the contemplative wisdom process. It begins a healing of the divorce-alienation.)

5. God's Presence in the Prayer of Frustration-Peace

The aim of the enemy's attack is to keep the alienated person from experiencing the presence of God in her life, to make
her feel damned. The aim of the Lord's wisdom process is to
make his presence ever more evident, to help the alienated person feel beloved. In the first instance, prayer and peace seem
impossible to gain. In the second instance, the contemplative

prayer of peace issuing out of a frustrating divorce-experience is happening; alienation is being healed. But so often in the midst of this frustration-peace prayer people ask: "How do I know that God loves me? It would give me so much confidence if I knew this were the case. Then I could live better with this divorce."

A person can know that God loves him or her. There are interior and exterior criteria which, when converged, yield confidence that God loves one. These criteria are especially needed when one feels alienated and is not enjoying that quasi-direct experience of God sometimes given in prayer. Let us glance at the interior criteria first:

(a) Experiencing a strong desire to serve God and his people well and feeling an enlarging openness to the previously feared situation. (Once I went to an inner city meeting of the Chicago Contract Buyers' League and heard one of the board members say: "I don't huddle up in my apartment no more; I'm out there on the street now, organizing people. We're fighting those banks and rich cats who hold those killing mortgages over our heads all these years. And the good Lord's given me the strength to do this; I ain't doing it by my lonesome, you can be sure of that.")

(b) Feeling a longing hunger for God as the center of my world, as the one who gives meaning to my life. (I was a chaplain in a hospital and visiting a certain notorious lady about sixty years of age who said to me: "Sonny, I've been through a lot and seen it all. Now I finally know who my God is and he's certainly different from the preacher's God of fire and brimstone. He takes care of me now and lets me know I'm not all bad. I have a hankering to see him soon if only to thank him for what these sisters here have done for me. They make me feel like I'm more than a wrinkled pow-derpuff picked up in the alley.")

(c) Wanting to be poor with Christ poor in his people, expe-riencing a being "at home with them." (I asked a mission-ary friend from a well-to-do family what he found attractive in his Bolivian mission. He answered, "Well, I go into a slum hut and offer the eucharist with the parents of four children. They invite me to supper and I watch them cut the lone bread-slab into seven pieces, each piece smaller because I stayed. But they are laughing, telling stories, and making me feel as though I was part of the family. This is the happiest moment of my life and it gets repeated almost every week.")

(d) Having a sense of hope even when those around one are depressed at the latest disaster. (The board member of the Contract Buyers' League again: "We haven't won a single case yet against the mortgage holders. But I don't put my trust in any court or judge; my trust is in the Lord. Still I'm going to use that court or judge as much as I can. You never can tell; we might just meet a good judge.")

(e) Feeling courage where ordinarily a person might cave in. (Being a thoroughgoing coward, I dreaded facing fifteen Jesuits and telling them that their program seemed against the spirit of Ignatius. It took me a month to write the letter, and with fear and trembling I went to the meeting which had been called to deal with my charge. At the meeting I was told how angry my letter had made some of them and why my judgment was hardly trustworthy. Though ordinarily I would have felt crushed, this time I felt serene about myself and strong in my charge. It was clear to me that the presence of the Lord—the serenity and strength— was never more tangible for me. This made it possible for me, though feeling the alienation, not to let the feeling divorce me from my fellow Jesuits. It was the Lord's doing, certainly not mine.)

(f) Deepening of gratitude for God's answering my every request though he does it in his own way for my greater good. (The more I work with elderly people who are close to God the more I am struck that what marks their life as holy is their constant gratitude. Very little of their life escapes this thankfulness—even the pains which they endure and the limitations [loss of memory, incontinence, financial dependency] which humiliate them. And gratitude is what heals the divorce they may feel from the young, the healthy, the busily successful, the do-gooders, and those who treat them like children. It is this same gratitude which keeps them reaching out to warm the hearts of others.)

These interior criteria must, of course, be balanced by and converge with exterior criteria if one is to know that God loves him or her in the midst of alienations. These latter criteria are among the following:

(a) The gift of friends whom the Lord has sent into one's life to enrich it with their talents, insights, affection, loyalty, joys and sufferings. (I resented that I had begun spiritual direction of others under the command of obedience and not by my own choice. Over the next fifteen years this resentment went underground but nevertheless plagued my work. Then, during a retreat, it struck me how fortunate I had been in having these directees. They had taught me prayer, thoughtfulness, humor amid distress, loyalty, the beauty of suffering for those one loves, and then offered me friendship—God's finest gift.)

(b) The Lord's unique providential care for a person as he rescues one from sins, foolish decisions, selfishness, and meanness—a pattern more and more recognizable over the years as he renders one more and more lovable to others. (This is the advantage of reaching one's sixties: the pattern of one's life becomes clearer. One recognizes that God has a way of drawing good out of one's most miserable mistakes such as the unjust punishment of a favorite daughter, out of a personal tragedy such as the early death of one's husband, out of bad luck such as the loss of one's job due to the "take-over" of the company.)

(c) The people whom God has entrusted to our parenting, guidance, teaching, and love. (The board member of the Contract Buyers' League once again: "I walked out of the auditorium after my son's high school graduation and five people came up to me and said: 'Jamey Johnston, I know you even though you don't know me—thanks a lot for fighting for us in the court even when we're too scared to fight alongside you.' It made me feel real good.'')

If a good number of these criteria are part of a person's everyday life, then God is present with him or her even if the feeling of alienation remains strong. The fact of reconciliation can co-exist with the lingering feeling of alienation. The contemplative prayer of frustration-peace is happening between this person and God even though the frustration clouds over the sun shining deep within the person. To understand this, one must note the diverse levels of peace within one's experience.

The first level is the sensuous where one experiences itching, cool breezes, smell of fresh baked bread, relaxation of laughter, chills, clang of a bell, taste of pizza. This is the superficial tissue of events which gives continuity to life.

The second level is the physical (underlying the minor irritations and pleasures of the first level) where lie the pain of ulcers and the exuberance of good health, the satisfaction of an expert tennis game or of a Verdi opera, the drum-beat of sexual pleasure or throbbing tension. These are the longer-lasting and more intense pleasures and pains which compenetrate the sensuous first level.

The third level is the psychic (more demanding and powerful than the second level) where operate the feeling of jeopardy at possible job loss, the sense of well-being because of being loved deeply by another, the hope of finally getting one's college degree, the fear of death, the satisfaction of completing successfully a four year experiment with a vaccine. These are the perduring inner events which give meaning to the two upper levels of experience and control one's attitudes toward people, hard luck, the world of work, and family values.

The fourth level is the mysterious (known only by comparison and contrast with the upper three levels) where God is most present like some great underground river nourishing all the life above it with its own life and stabilizing all the fluctuations above it with its staying power, yet hidden from view until one explores for it out of dissatisfaction with the upper levels.[5]

Peace, then, can be defined in four different ways: sensuous satisfaction of the first level, pleasurable joy of the second level, beatific fulfillment of the third level, the sense of God present to all one's joys and sufferings at the fourth level. This fourth level of peace, a continuing rightness with God, can be strong in the midst of alienating divorce at the third level, poor health at the second level, and irritations at the first level. It can also transform those upper levels with its nourishing and stabilizing influence so that we can keep healthily balanced amid the topsy-turvy life of constant interruptions, zany unpredictable events, and the storms of envy, shame, anger, sorrow, and pain which gust within us.

It is precisely through the wisdom process of conversion that one can become aware of this fourth-level peace (God's immediate, but obscure, presence). For this awareness happens to be the frustration-peace prayer whereby alienating divorce begins to heal under the warm benevolence of God's presence deep within one at this fourth level of experience. The greatest problem of life which we face, then, is to find the Prince of peace in our depths and to let him lovingly heal us of our alienations even as we walk through the desert of divorce and alienation.

Chapter Seven
Smoldering Anger at God

1. The Feel of Alienation from God: Homelessness

The feel of alienation from God is very often accompanied by felt estrangement from career, self, family, and friends. I look at my work as car mechanic or engineer or nurse or social worker or maintenance person and see it as shoddy. My skills are actually only half-used. So, I cheat my clients or customers precisely when I am trying to serve them—and these are God's people. At this point I experience the bitter anger of frustration with God. He has made me so limited and yet he is supposed to be provident for me. What do I have to offer him except my squandered past life, my present fumblings, and my blighted future? I feel imprisoned within my sins, faults, and limitations. The smoldering anger of frustration suddenly flames up out of my violent depression in a half-curse and a half-begging for help. I feel that I am totally unlovable and unloving. I walk through my day like a homeless waif who has learned to trust no one.

The Lord's demands seem impossible: "Whatever you do for the least of my brothers, you do for me." How can my family respect me when they look at my work-record or see me snarling at them because nothing seems to go right either at work or at home? They try to protect themselves by keeping a safe distance from me. Even my so-called spouse seems to be ill at ease when we sit around the dinner table. What does my family expect of me—total success, unstinting devotion, no moods, constant heroism? Are my friends that much better than I am? If they think they are better, then let them, too, keep a safe distance from me—especially if they call themselves Christians and think that they are God's special people. I am sick of the hypocrisy of church people. Let them all keep their distance.

So, I am cutting myself off from everybody. And why not
from God, too? How could he find time for the likes of me, the
"great sinner"? I am better off to pretend that he does not exist
and to find some things to do—anything that will keep my mind
off him and off myself. He is no better than a distant star, hard
as a diamond, bright as a klieg light, as he eyes me with his cold
eternal stare. He is uncaring, unperturbed, by my situation.
Why ever again try to pray to him? Prayer makes me feel even
more dull, routinized, mechanical than I am. God no longer has
a face. He is just an angry volcano in the sky, waiting to pour
blazing hot lava on me when my time comes—if he exists at all.

Amid this tirade of the God-alienated person, it could be
noted that the more alienated one is or feels from family,
friends, and work, the more alienated one is or feels from oneself. And the more self-alienated one is or feels, the more alienated one is or feels from the God present in oneself and in others. It is like a great triangle of mutual alienations, the opposite
of the two great commandments. No wonder the alienated
Christian constantly feels a smoldering anger in himself or herself. Yet at the same time he or she experiences a strong desire
to be reconciled, to be at home with self, others and God—a
God who likes and cares for him or her.

When feeling so deeply alienated, a person may be helped
by listening to someone else who is turning his agony of self-
distrust toward God:

> Before you no living man is just. For the enemy
> [Satan? Self? Another?] pursues me; he has crushed my
> life to the ground; he has left me dwelling in the dark
> like those long dead. And my spirit is faint within
> me. . . . I stretch out my hands to you; my soul thirsts
> for you like parched land. . . . Hide not your face from
> me. . . . At dawn let me hear of your kindness, for in
> you I trust (Ps 143:2–10).

Is there not some hope left? For "you know when I sit and
when I stand; you understand my thoughts from afar. . . . You
have formed my inmost being; you knit me in my mother's

womb" (Ps 139:2, 13). If only God would face me. If only I could face him.

2. The All-Too-Real Fact of Alienation from God

A. *The Changing Faces of God*

Unlike the gods of some religions, the Christian God knew we needed him to have a face and so he gave us Jesus. For the face reveals so much of the person: the flare of nostrils and the reddening complexion of anger, the staring eyes and trembling mouth of fear, the softened mouth and warm eyes of affection, the twisted lips and vinegar look of bitterness, the vacant gaze and slack mouth of despair. But the face of the beloved changes not only according to feelings but according to the aging process from dark to white hair, from smooth to wrinkled skin, from spare to ample shaping, from quick to slower smile, from sharp to warmer eyes. All these changes chronicle the joys and sufferings of life with the beloved.

It is no wonder, then, that as a child one sees the young Jesus bright, alert, fun-loving like oneself. Later in one's adolescence Jesus is seen as finding his way in the restrictive adult world of parents who are puzzled at his independence in the temple and who do not quite know what to make of him. As young adults we are intrigued by the competent Jesus ready to preach-work-heal but held up by the forty days in the desert. As middle-agers we find him being cynical about do-goodism and struggling to hold family, community and church together under cultural stresses. After sixty years we tend to find Jesus a bit tired yet persevering, wise and still hopeful. As, through the years, each of us battles with various types of alienation, we recognize better the many varieties of experience swirling within the personality of Jesus. How supple his facial expression.

The face of God also changes in the ecclesial community as down through the centuries the church deals with varying cultural pressures and estrangements. The early church saw the Lord as a concerned shepherd; for its pastoral and urban peoples lived in terrible jeopardy while the Roman empire was crumbling under the blows of the wandering Gothic hordes. During the Constantine-Charlemagne period, God had the stern face of an emperor God regnant amid the turmoil of a disintegrating Europe. The medieval period, preoccupied with death-hell-purgatory-heaven, offered us the divine face of a great austere judge to stimulate penitence amid the luxuries and wild exuberance of the new trade-routes and the crusades—the serenely omnipotent Pancrator of the Eastern church being an interesting counterpart of this. The agonizing crucified Jesus gave the Europe of the sixteenth to the nineteenth century a face which challenged its arrogant rationalism in all endeavors and its high optimism over its all-conquering science. Ten years before Vatican II, the face of a risen Christ rose into our consciousness—a face serene, humble, and hope-filled, amid the terrors of nuclear bombs, cold and hot wars, third world hunger and fourth world despair.

What will be the face of God for the year 2000? Will it include all of the previous faces or will it bring a new face into our consciousness? Will God face us as the rescuer from our sense of nothingness and homelessness? as the urban dweller at home with our scientific-technological society (more than the God of farms and nature)? as the comforting and "always-at-home-for-us" God of the expelled peoples who are alienated from almost the whole universe?

God's face, then, seems to change according to the estrangements which confront his beloved spouse, the church. But despite his totally identifying with us and with our needs, we can be quite partial, even alienated, in responding to our trinitarian God. Because of the distant and domineering face of one's natural father, one can tune the Father out while concentrating all attention on the Son. Or if one closely associates the Spirit with a caricatured charismatic movement, with overly enthusiastic "weirdos" and with a childish intepretation of dove-fire-wind, one can have time only for the Father whom one considers more conservative. Or if one centers attention only upon the restrictive, seemingly harsh demands of the Father or if one fears that falling in love with Christ inevitably means sexual complications, then one can experience alienation from Son and Father and seek safety under the wings of the Spirit.

One's selectivity among the persons of the Trinity, then, may be simply a transfer to the face of God of some hidden anger or fright or irritation or disgust felt in daily human encounters. In this way, alienation is a basic ingredient of prayer life just as it is of the whole Bible. I need time to understand and patience to abandon my alienating image of God (which is remarkably like my own self-image) and to reconcile myself to the real God. In prayer, the Lord can gradually change my image of him—if I allow him the freedom to do so.

Here it is important to realize that God is not hurt by my alienation, though he does experience it with me and does suffer for me (not because of me). Through Jeremiah (7:18), Yahweh says just this:

> The children gather wood, their fathers light the fire, and the women knead the dough to make cakes for the queen of heaven [the Assyro-Babylonian Ishtar, goddess of fertility] while libations are poured out to strange gods in order to hurt me. Is it I whom they hurt, says the Lord; is it not rather themselves to their own confusion?

I may be hurt through a chosen or unchosen alienation. If chosen, I objectively hurt only myself and those dear to me; if unchosen, I suffer the feeling of alienation but objectively I hurt no one, not even myself though I feel hurt. In either case, God suffers with me and for me in my suffering but is not hurt by me. Meanwhile my very image of God can make me angrily distant from him.

B. *The Primitive Source of All Alienation: Original Sin*

Beneath any alienating image of God and deeper than any factual or merely felt alienation is the ultimate source of all alienations, namely, original sin. The latter is a mysterious state of the world which deeply affects my image of and relation with

God. Without revelation (particularly the first three chapters of Genesis and the fifth chapter of St. Paul's letter to the Romans), we would know only that "something has gone wrong in the past to hurt us tragically now"—the shared insight of an Albert Camus and a John Henry Newman.

But by revelation we discover the garden of Eden standing for the whole world, a world very different from our present one. In the Eden world, humans had a more immediate experience of God; in the cool of the evening they would go walking with Yahweh (Gen 3:8).[1] And so there were no lies, no revolts, no violence; rather there was an assurance of being loved deeply by God. As a result life was full, joyous, wholesome, and direct from God's hand. This does not mean that primitive man had mastered his world. Indeed, he could be coarse and ignorant as well as be imperiled by wild animals, lightning, earthquakes, and floods.

Because of God's immediacy to him, however, he obeyed God gladly and worked hard to gradually complete God's creation through the use of synthetic contemplation. For this reason, he enjoyed four special gifts to which he was not strictly entitled: wholesomeness, knowledge, impassibility, and immortality. Wholesomeness meant that he was not torn by conflicting desires but only drawn by the tension of wanting God more and more in his life. Though he had much less information about the world than most contemporary persons, still, through the gift of knowledge, he knew better than we moderns whatever he grasped of reality. In other words, he found God in each thing easily by way of analytic contemplation.

For the simple reason that man had an extended body of extremely delicate susceptibility, he could be cut and bruised in accidents and could contract illnesses. Yet by the gift of impassibility his pain or sickness at one level of experience did not cause him suffering at a higher level of consciousness since God was so immediately present to him. Finally the fourth gift of immortality did *not* mean that he could not die since the biological aging process would under any circumstances wear man's earthly body down to bare subsistence. But this gift did mean that there would be no fear of death. Instead, the dying person would feel a strong calm desire to be more fully with God who was to resurrect his body before its dissolution. This was the Eden world.

Then for some mysterious reason, man said "no" to God in a very important decision. Man wanted to be independent of God, to be himself a god, and said equivalently: "I will no longer companion you in obedience." Like a lethal atomic cloud this rebellion spread among all humans; no one escaped it. Was the cause pride, specious liberty, a restless dissatisfaction with God's future plans? No one knows. But one result was evident: the loss of man's four special gifts. Fiercely conflicting longings began to tear apart man's wholesomeness, prejudice and pretense rose out of ignorance, pain turned into suffering, dying became an agonizing experience. Out of false righteousness, the anger of resentment possessed man's being as though God, not himself, were the culprit causing his new state. A second result was man's felt need for some special strength to live in this new after-Eden world. He had lost the more immediate presence of God; this was his original righteousness and holiness as the Council of Trent puts it.

Only the coming of God the Son into our history could save us from unending disaster. For he took on our suffering and death. Then, through his resurrection, he raised us out of our sins to the Father. In rescuing us, he restored our wholeness (the gifts of the Holy Spirit sent by Father and Son), our knowledge (the risen Jesus as revelation itself) and our attitudes (the lived values of faith, hope and charity) so that we could once again consciously yield to the immediate, yet now obscure, presence of God. This is Jesus' dynamic act of redemption which more than compensates for our tragic losses due to original sin (Rom 5:15). Now awareness of the indwelling Trinity (as revealed in John's last supper account) is again stimulated and the radical prayer found in analytic and synthetic contemplation again becomes possible. Through this reconciliation process we can now overcome the ultimate source of all alienation.

But precisely what is this original sin revealed to us in scripture, the fathers, and the councils?[2] In the Old Testament there is no clear-cut concept of original sin. But there is certainly an awareness of sin (Gen 6:12) and chapters 4 to 11 of Genesis show the death and destruction following upon original sin.[3] It is St. Paul who describes original sin through its effects on us (Rom 5:12–21). Because of Adam's act of arrogance, we are sinners without spirit. But because of Christ, we are sought out by God who offers us grace for the asking. Our state of being without spirit and yet of having grace made available to us precedes any free decision we might make to accept or to reject the grace of the spirit.

In other words, original sin in me has not been caused by my own personal sinning; it is something that happens in me because of others' previous personal sins. Yet every human (except Christ's mother) is headed for death because of the solidarity of the human community in these sins. "We are all in this together." By turning to Christ for help and by trying with all my heart not to sin, I become liberated from my sinfulness (Rom 6:1–23) and rise to a new style of living with Christ (1 Cor 15:3, 17; Gal 1:4). Nevertheless, the conflict between my spirit and my sensual desires persists till death (Rom 8:1–17).

St. Augustine of Hippo, taking hold of St. Paul's explanation of what original sin is, crystalizes its meaning for us. He takes Paul's term, concupiscence (the experience of evil), and declares it to be a person's spontaneous desire for sensual satisfaction—a desire which precedes and enters into every deed one performs. As Pierre Grelot notes, this is to experience one's very existence as coarse, as suffering, as destined for death, as torn by an ambivalent conscience, as incapable of doing the good desired, and as secretly cooperative with an evil which is at once attractive and repulsive.[4] This experience is so strong in us that we, like Augustine, could be tempted to think that concupiscence is original sin when actually, according to St. Thomas Aquinas and the Council of Trent, concupiscence is simply the effect of original sin. For the essence of original sin is, according to St. Anselm, the lack of sanctifying grace (original justice or righteous holiness).

Contemporary theologians are agreed that original sin is not simply the sinful act of Adam, nor simply our resultant collective guilt felt in concupiscence. Rather, it is basically a lack of holiness which precedes any personal decisions and modifies them when we put them into action. This is a *state* of alienation for which no one of us contemporaries is personally responsible. But theologians add that, before any of our personal decisions come to be, a certain state of holiness is also present in us. This latter state consists of two factors: God's communication of himself to every human being and our corresponding desire to seek him out wherever he may be. We are, then, ready for reconciliation at all times and places even while in this vast state of alienation.

Clearly, original sin was not God's plan for us. We humans introduced it and God adapted his plan to our willfulness. Consequently, the Father sent Jesus into our lives so that, through baptism in Christ, sanctifying grace and the dynamic presence of the indwelling Trinity could enter into this state of holiness to render us Christians ready for gospel-living. In this way we achieve basic reconciliation with God and others. Then our smoldering anger at supposed injustice can be quenched.

All this becomes very real and historical if one looks at both the interior and exterior situation of present-day human living amid original sin. Interiorly, our decision for or against Christ is under the impact of concupiscence and death which say to us: "Don't worry about God or others. Live it up because tomorrow you may be dead." Exteriorly, our free actions in the world either approve this worldly life through self-centered concupiscence or sponsor the Christian life of other-centered sacrifice through faith, hope and charity.

Amid this ambivalence, our forefathers' and foremothers' free decisions, when corrupted by concupiscence, gave rise to the "sinful structures of society." Such are the traditional policies of grafting and bribery in political and business life, the proliferation of wars, economic exploitation of the poor, abuse of the right to life in abortions and euthanasia, men's domination of women, genial enslavement of the fourth world to the first world, and the decline of family fidelity in divorce and in child abuse. Matthew (24:10–13) puts it succinctly: "Many will falter, betraying and hating one another. False prophets will arise in great numbers to mislead many. Because of the increase of evil, the love of most will grow cold. The man who holds out to the end, however, is the one who will see salvation.''

All this is social alienation. For, through these evil institutions, the downtrodden people or society's losers see their chances of a better life disappear far into the future and feel that no one cares. They are distanced from their hopes, from the people who could help them and from their own sense of dignity. Under their despair smolders the fierce anger of felt injustice. For these alienating structures of society are not simply the product of original sin; they are also strengthened cunningly by the free decisions of contemporary people who connive with original sin. They are the result of personal sin, a second universal source of alienation.

C. The Major Contemporary Source of Alienation: Personal Sin

Personal sin, too, is a mystery which only revelation can clarify. Whole cultures have failed to see sin for what it is. They consider it simply a mistake (the Greeks) or merely an act unworthy of a person's dignity (Confucian society); they fail to recognize it as an affront to God as well as an attack on a fellow human being. For this reason, the crucifixion of Christ is merely a ghastly event, not a revelation of the horror of sin committed against God and his people, not a magnificently generous act of reconciliation. Paul informs and cautions his Colossians (1:19–23) about Christ's rescue of us:

> It pleased God to make absolute fullness reside in him and, by means of him, to reconcile everything in his person, both on earth and in the heavens, making peace through the blood of his cross. You yourselves were once alienated from him; you nourished hostility in your hearts because of your evil deeds. But now Christ has achieved reconciliation for you in his mortal body by dying so as to present you to God holy, free

of reproach and blame. But you must hold fast to faith
. . . unshaken in the hope promised you by the gospel.

The blood of God is the price of personal sin and of its worldwide reconciliation. Sin is no mere mistake, not simply gauche
behavior. Its flinty injustice strikes up the smoldering anger
which burns not only against evil-doers but also mistakenly
against the God who seems to take no action against the
injustice.

Sin is also three-dimensional. It is, first of all, self-alienat-
ing, self-degrading, eventually self-annihilating. Paul describes
this:

> You must no longer live as the pagans do—their minds
> empty, their understanding darkened. They are
> estranged from a life in God because of their ignorance
> and their resistance; without remorse they have aban-
> doned themselves to lust and the indulgence of every
> sort of lewd conduct. . . . You must lay aside your for-
> mer way of life and old self which deteriorates through
> illusion and desire, and . . . put on the new man cre-
> ated in God's image whose justice and holiness are
> born of truth (Eph 4:17–24).

Sin is at least tragic for the sinner. Without Christ his situation
is hopeless.

Second, sin is against the God who is in us and in the people around us. It is God-alienating. The Lord cautions us
through Jeremiah: "Be warned lest I be estranged from
you. . . . Small and great alike, all are greedy for gain . . . they
know not how to blush. . . . See, I bring evil upon this people,
the fruit of their own schemes, because they heeded not my
words, because they despised my law" (Jer 6:8–19). I, the sinner, attack God's graceful presence in us all and incidentally
worsen the situation for all others by adding to its evil.

This I do through betrayal of family, friends, acquaintances, and people whom I am meant to serve with my God-
given talents for business, sports, journalism, home-making,

law, and so on. I refuse to believe and to act on the fact that "as often as you did it for one of my least brothers, you did it for me [Christ]" (Mt 25:40). Our God so identifies himself with our fellow human beings that to touch them with reverence or irreverence is to touch him in this same way. Here is the third dimension of sin, the alienation and degradation of others who are dear to the Lord. He has good reason to be angry at this.

If one should doubt the reality of sin, he or she has only to look into the eyes of the rape-victim, of the abused child, of the person robbed and beaten, of the gossip-victim, of the person betrayed by a supposed friend. Then Paul's remarks about lying, cheating, revenging, cheating on the job, slandering and mean bullying take on a new poignancy (Eph 4:25–32). For, on looking into the eyes of his victim, the sinner sees his own twisted face, the victim's hurt and despair, and God within the depths of that despairing hurt.

Such sinning is mortal when I set not only my action but also myself directly against God's plan. For then I set myself up as more important than God or anyone else. I consider myself as self-made and as answering to no one except myself. This is a basic, hard-to-revoke choice which enters into and controls all my other actions. I establish my kingdom, no matter how small, against God's kingdom. I pretend to own this world by my own right. God help anyone who challenges my right; he or she will feel my searing anger. I am mortally wounding myself again and again and again.

This is quite different from venial sin whereby I set only my action, not myself also, against God. Here I do not want to challenge God and to establish my own kingdom, even though I am beginning to do so if I persist in this way of life. Such venial sin becomes serious sin when I cause significant damage to another; yet even then I may protest that I am not setting up a counter-kingdom to Christ's. Thus the anger of self-righteousness is less virulent here than in mortal sin. As a result, we discover various grades of alienation due to the complexity of a situation and of our human motivation. This is the personal alienation which arises out of the ultimate source of all alienation, original sin.

3. The Faith Response to Alienation:
Reconciliation out of Hope, Service to Others, and True Guilt

A. *Hope Is Within Our Very Being*

There is, however, solid hope for reconciliation in the midst of the worst sinfulness. First of all, the human being has a radical capacity for grace. Here is that positive holiness which, alongside of original sin, precedes any human action. What is this? It is not something added on to the human spirit. Rather, it is a permanent quality within the human being which orients his or her spirit toward the God of grace. Indeed, it works within the natural desire for God since human existence itself is made for God and keeps us forever restless to find and possess him. But it is not grace itself. Instead, it is a wide welcome to all beings and ultimately to God, a radical source of reconciliation. It is a kind of assurance of unmerited grace and enables the spirit later freely to accept or to reject the actual offer of grace.[5]

A second reason for hope is that the human being is free and therefore self-possessed and aware of his or her dignity. A negative measure of this self-worth is a person's ability to say "no" to God and to make this decision stand forever. Within limits, therefore, the human being decides who he or she will become. Such freedom develops into mature liberty when the person attains such integration of intelligence, virtues, skills, and emotions that he or she can choose the good (even the better) consistently. Of course, this integration is enhanced enormously by the assistance of Christ's grace, but it is also the natural development of the full human personality. This is why a person literally is her liberty because she becomes the sum total of her previous free decisions made under the gracious unifying influence of Christ.

A third reason for hope is the sheer faithfulness of the Lord. This is a favorite theme of St. Paul: "It is precisely in this that God proves his love for us: that while we were still sinners, Christ died for us" (Rom 5:8). Again: "If we are unfaithful, he will still remain faithful, for he cannot deny himself" (2 Tim 2:13), that is, he is faithfulness itself. Nor do we merit this faithfulness; it is sheer gift from faithfulness itself:

> We went our way in malice and envy, hateful ourselves and hating one another. But when the kindness and love of God our savior appeared, he saved us; not because of any righteous deeds we had done, but because of his mercy. He saved us through the baptism of new birth and renewal by the Holy Spirit. This Spirit he lavished on us through Jesus Christ our Savior, that we might be justified by his grace and become heirs, in hope, of eternal life (Tit 3:3–7).

The Father gives us without reserve the Holy Spirit to be the living hope within us. As a result, reconciliation is within our very being if we should need it. Under these circumstances, anger at God appears foolish. Nevertheless, we are at times foolish, even though we have deep hope in God's ability to reconcile us with himself, others and our own selves.

B. Service of Others in Faith

Such startling generosity on God's part lures us into serving others with the same faithfulness with which God serves us. John of the letters (1 Jn 4:10–11) puts it to us bluntly: "Love, then, consists in this: not that we have loved God, but that he has loved us [first] and has sent his Son as an offering for our sins. Beloved, if God has loved us so, we must have the same love for one another." John thinks that God's love for us is so contagious that, having caught his love, we cannot but love our neighbor as generously as God has loved us. Such service of others will seem "natural" to us as a response to God's healing of our alienations. But why is this so?

First of all, we have all had the experience of loving a particular person and of finding it, therefore, much easier to love the family of that person. Somehow the radical love a person has for James branches out in love for his wife Eileen, their two sons Jeff and Tommy, and their daughter Jessica. To change the metaphor, love like hate is contagious; it can move out from one member of a family to embrace the whole family. Then, love or hate will naturally break out into actions of either service or disservice to the beloved and to his or her family. This is how we seem to mysteriously operate for reconciliation or for greater alienation.

But in the case of God, the direction of reconciliation may work differently. Once one embraces the whole which is God, one finds oneself embracing all his "parts," namely, Jesus, Mary, Joseph, the apostles, the members of one's own family, fellow workers, friends, and even acquaintances. This is simply the way of love.[6] It seems to happen similarly in a family established in love. For example, in loving his whole family altruistically, the father ends up loving himself since his family gives that basic meaning to life around which he builds his personality. Further, as he notes the resemblance of his daughters to his beloved wife, they become more precious to him; he also is secretly pleased to see his son taking up the sports he loves and acting with the generosity he admires toward his two sisters and mother. His pride in the whole family is made up of the pride he takes in each member. This wholesome love of each and all the family members enables him to serve them wholeheartedly, even to death if need be. Here is familial reconciliation at its strongest against any divorce or favoritism or disloyalty toward only one member. Is it not also the way of ecclesial reconciliation where the love of God enables one to embrace the whole congregation even though some members irritate one notably?

Such natural family-love opens out into the gospel love of the Trinity where the praying person loves God as a whole, i.e. without selective alienation from one or other of the persons and with a desire to see this divine family well served in its totality. This totality, of course, includes Jesus, the Son of God who also became the Son of Man. For this reason, in seeing Jesus, one sees the Father (Jn 14:8–10; 12:45) and, in hating Jesus, one hates the Father (Jn 15:23). So close is their union that factual (not merely feeling) alienation from one is alienation from the other. The same is true for the Holy Spirit who will speak only what he hears, and will announce to you the things to come. In doing this he will give glory to me [Christ], because he will have received from me what he will announce to you. All that the Father has belongs to me. That is why I said that what he [the Spirit] will announce to you he will have from me (Jn 16:13–15).

In other words, the three persons each share *totally* the one infinite divine being so that each acts out of the total Godhead. For this reason, factual alienation from or reconciliation with the Holy Spirit results in factual alienation from or reconciliation with the Father and the Son.

This union enables the Son in Jesus to reveal the inner life of the Father through Jesus' very service of the people of God. Jesus' embracing of the children reveals the Father blessing them; his touching of the leper is the Father's compassion surging through Jesus; his enjoying of Matthew's party for the tax collector's friends is the Father's delight in his children's happiness; his defending of Magdalene's generosity after she anointed him is also the Father's loving care for the outcast; his suffering of the passion reveals not only his own hiddenness and vulnerability but also that of the Father.

One's union with and imaging of Jesus in daily living works similarly to that of Jesus, the perfect image of the Father. I am naturally the central reference for all my actions and I therefore necessarily see any scene according to my self-image since the latter acts as the context for any observation I make. Thus, if I image myself as a child of God and as the brother of Christ, I tend to see others the same way as I see myself. When, therefore, I regularly see others as children of God and brothers or sisters of Jesus, I "naturally" want to serve them. Like Jesus whom I image, I am guided by his servant attitude in alerting others to God's kingdom. My self-image includes service of God's people. This ensures a practical and warm reconciliation.

After Jesus had washed the feet of his apostles, he pointed out how central to his life and to theirs was servanthood: "You must wash each other's feet. What I just did was to give you an example; as I have done, so you must do" (Jn 13:14–15). Can Christ's service of people along with the Father have no effect on our reconciling work with the same people? Will not this union of the Father and Jesus enter into our faith-filled attempts to reconcile people to the Father through Jesus? Does not our own service of others in the image of the servant Jesus, then, become the source of reconciliation for the whole divine family with the universal human family?

A startling response to these questions is the story of the woman at Jacob's well (Jn 4:4–42). Despite her apparently bad experience in her five previous marriages and in her present liaison, she continued to believe in God and refused to live in a hard shell of bitterness. Her quick wit remained sharp, her mind kept open to new experiences, her heart was still ready to love even when hurt. So, when Jesus unexpectedly asked for water from her, a Samaritan and a woman, she did not seal him off. Instead, she asked penetrating questions and received matching answers.

Then Jesus suddenly broke through her defenses with a seemingly harsh remark about her sexual life. But her heart, aware of how he respected her, was ready to accept his invitation to proclaim his messiahship to the townspeople. This was no doubt quite embarrassing for her and it eventuated in her rejection as Jesus' first apostle when the townspeople arrogantly informed her: "No longer does our faith depend on your story. We have heard for ourselves and we know that this really is the savior of the world." Like Mary Magdalene, she too had loved much and now knew well both the beautiful and the harsh meaning of being a servant for God's people.

Perhaps the words of St. Paul would eventually be some consolation to her: "All this [the new creation] has been done by God, who has reconciled us to himself through Christ, and has given us the ministry of reconciliation. . . . This makes us ambassadors for Christ; God as it were appealing through us" (2 Cor 5:18–20). She had imaged well the servant Jesus in her ambassadorship. Would this mission of reconciling people to the Father through Jesus ever be taken from her?

Like Jesus, the Holy Spirit, through his service within and

outside the church, reveals the inner life of the Father and "incidentally" of the Son. The Spirit serves, first of all, within the disciples, indeed within the woman at Jacob's well. Jesus says in his last testament: "I will ask the Father and he will give you another Paraclete [besides Jesus] to be with you always" (Jn 14:16), "[to] instruct you in everything and [to] remind you of all that I told you" (Jn 14:26), "[to] bear witness on my behalf. You must bear witness as well" (Jn 15:26–27).

The Holy Spirit, then, unites himself to the disciples of the first and twentieth centuries as they bear witness to Jesus through serving his people. In this way, the church or earthly family of God is living the Spirit of Jesus, the Holy Spirit. Not only is the Spirit revealed to others through the actions of Christians, but also the inner life of Jesus and, hence, of the Father becomes known to those served in our very ministry. This is most dramatically seen in the Christian mother's and father's care for their children and for each other.

Because of this unified service in and to the world, both individual and social reconciliation begin to happen—individual insofar as each Christian becomes more united to the Spirit of Jesus; social insofar as the commonly shared Spirit of Jesus unites the Christian community within itself and with the people served by the community. This faithful service, then, becomes the basic response to the world's many levels of alienation. For it is charismatic (Spirited) in its adaptability to the world's needs and hopes. Yet it is also institutionally organized according to Christ, the logos, in order that it may minister with continual fidelity to these same needs and hopes. Further, it is established solidly and energized widely by the always creating Father. How can such service fail to reconcile the world to God?

Indeed, the Acts of the Apostles, often called the gospel of the Holy Spirit, describes in detail how the Christian community's life reveals the Holy Spirit's identity through its reconciling apostolic service. At Pentecost "all were filled with the Holy Spirit. They began to express themselves in foreign tongues and to make bold proclamation as the Spirit prompted them" (Acts 2:4). "Those who accepted his [Peter's] message

were baptized; some three thousand were added that day"
(Acts 2:41). After the cure of the cripple at the Beautiful Gate,
the subsequent conversion of five thousand more people, the
consequent arrest of Peter and John, and their appearance
before the Sanhedrin, "Peter, filled with the Holy Spirit, spoke
up. . . . 'It [the cure] was done in the name of Jesus Christ the
Nazorean whom you crucified and whom God raised from the
dead'" (Acts 4:8–10).

The Holy Spirit, the Spirit of truth, was intimate to the disciples' lives of reconciling service so that when Ananias embezzled the funds of the community, Peter could say: "Ananias,
why have you let Satan fill your heart so as to make you lie to
the Holy Spirit and keep for yourself some of the proceeds from
that field?" (Acts 5:3). The community is not only bonded but
also energized to service by the Holy Spirit through the laying
on of hands amid remarkable signs and wonders (Acts 8:13–
15). Hence, Philip the deacon is told by the Spirit to catch up
to the carriage of the Ethiopian, Queen Candace's treasurer,
for converting him and then is later snatched away for other
work by the same Spirit (Acts 8:27–29, 39).

While Peter was still pondering his vision of the canvas let
down from the sky and before he had even thought of giving
the good news to the Gentiles, "the Spirit said to him: 'There
are two men in search of you. Go downstairs and set out with
them unhesitatingly, for it is I who sent them'" (Acts 10:19–
20). After his arrival at the house of the Gentile Cornelius and
while Peter was evangelizing the family, "the Spirit descended
upon all who were listening to Peter's message. The circum-
cised believers who had accompanied Peter were surprised that
the gift of the Holy Spirit should have been poured out on the
Gentiles also" (Acts 10:44–45; cf. also 11:15–18). Apparently
the Spirit's idea of reconciling service was a bit more generous
than the Jewish believers' conception.

Finally, during a liturgy, "the Holy Spirit spoke to them:
'Set apart Barnabas and Saul for me to do the work for which I
have called them'" (Acts 13:2). Here began the four great missionary journeys of Paul to convert the peoples of the Mediterranean basin, the whole then-known world. Thus did the Holy

Spirit inspire and unite the faith-filled reconciling service of Jesus' embryonic church. What is particularly remarkable here is that this faithful service of and with the Holy Spirit happens despite the alienations, e.g., between Jewish and Gentile Christians, between Peter and Paul, between Barnabas and Paul, between Peter and the ambitious sons of Zebedee. In fact, the ugliness of these very alienations contrasts sharply with the beauty and strength of their later conversion by the Holy Spirit into perduring reconciliations. This is the mark of faithful service.

But the revealing of the Holy Spirit in the Acts of the Apostles is rooted in the gospels. There the Holy Spirit achieved in the womb of Mary the ultimate reconciliation of God and man in Jesus, there the Holy Spirit filled Mary with the exuberance of the Magnificat for the trip to and care of Elizabeth, there the Holy Spirit healed the bruised spirits of Joseph and Mary for reconciliation and marriage, there the Spirit presided over Jesus' joyful baptism and first gathering of disciples (Jn 1), there the Spirit was breathed into the disciples in that second gathering of the disciples after his resurrection.

Could it be that the Spirit's basic service is to foster acquaintances, next to build friendships out of them, and then to fashion the family of God out of these friendships—and all this through the enspirited sacraments, the inspired word of God and spiritual discernment? Is this not apostolic reconciliation which is responding to the deep and constant alienations occurring in contemporary society? Is this not the greatest service we Christians can offer to the world? And is not such service based on the Christian hope within us? If this be so, why is this reconciliation not more successful? What cripples it?

C. The Empire of False Guilt

There are some who claim that pride is the crippling source of most alienations. Others point to the bitterness of vanity or of jealousy or of rejected love. Some years of experience tempt me to say that, among good-willed people, the greatest source of alienation from God and from service of others is false guilt. To understand this, it is necessary, first of all, to note what guilt is and to discover how mysteriously it works in us.

Guilt is a signal of loss. It is a pain one feels at some degrading act like self-depreciation or cowardice or failure to defend a friend or dereliction of duty as doctor, counselor, mother, or teacher. It is a sense of being blameworthy.[7] The resultant disappointment with oneself leads to vain regret, then anger at oneself and finally depression. Yet guilt itself is not depression even though its persistence can cause depression if the cause of guilt is not faced honestly. Nor is guilt simply frustration, nor is it fatigue, nor is it disenchantment with someone or with some personal decision, even though all these factors can be present at a time of guilt.

What makes guilt hard to assess is its two-sidedness. Subjective guilt is the *feeling* of shame, embarrassment, and sorrow arising out of one's estimate that one has denied a cherished self-chosen life-value. For example, I feel shame over neglecting a favorite aunt while claiming that family values are paramount for me. On the other hand, objective guilt is my *actual living* in contradiction of my values and truth convictions, e.g. I truly do put everything else ahead of visiting my aunt.

Another complication is that the pain of guilt occurs at different levels of our experience. The first level of pain is the physical, e.g. a toothache, a stomach-ulcer twinge, the headache of a brain-tumor. The second level is the psychological, e.g. sorrow at an insult endured, loneliness of isolation, grief at losing one's job. At the third or spiritual level, pain comes at a death of a friend, at a sense of life being wasted on trifles, at a failure to live up to family-expectations, or at a fear that God actually dislikes me. Now subjective guilt occurs only at the psychological and spiritual levels even though it gets expressed at the physical level in the blush, the downcast eyes, and the half-hearted action. The intertwined pains at the psychological and spiritual levels are subjective guilt which is caused by some objective event outside the person such as job-loss due to laziness, the freezing of a once warm friendship through neglect, or a mean sin against someone dear. These outside events wherein I actually live contrary to my values and convictions are objective guilt.

Because of the distinctness of subjective and objective guilt, one can have a feeling of guilt without any basis in fact. This is called false guilt, a feeling of blameworthiness generated when a person falsely accuses himself of an act or of an event for which he is not truly responsible. For example, without any neglect on her part, a daughter arrives late for her mother's death and *feels* guilty about this; a son refuses to have his unconscious father of eighty years go through a colostomy to give him another two months of life (or of prolonged death) and *feels* guilty about this; a child has a spat with her mother in the morning and *feels* guilty when in the evening the mother suffers a mild heart-attack. This false guilt is what the psychiatrist tries to lift off the shoulders of a patient lest it crush him or her.

True guilt, on the other hand, is a feeling of blameworthiness when a mother is truly neglectful of her daughter's need for parental counseling or when an administrator truly gossips about a secretary to her office manager so that she is not promoted. In true guilt I have factually sinned against another and thus have degraded my own self. That is, I have lessened the good in myself and damaged the other so that I (and perhaps the other) am less compassionate, less loyal, more vengeful, more prone to lie. In other words, I have become less a person and have given the other the opportunity to become less.

Such a sin, such an evil fact of life, rightly generates the feeling of guilt. True guilt, unlike false guilt, is psychologically and spiritually healthy because this feeling accurately reflects a person's involvement in behavior contrary to his or her self-chosen life-values. The feeling of true guilt reveals the evil situation as it really is. The wise counselor, then, does not help the patient hide true guilt but rather helps him or her discover it.

For these reasons, loss of a sense of true guilt is dangerous because this means that the guilty person is failing to see the reality of evil in the self and in others. Laughing at sin is like the death rattle of one's personhood. I can try to hide my sin and true guilt under nonchalant excuses for my behavior: "My parents are responsible for my selfishness, everyone else is cheating on the expense account, God made me this way, my sins are simply exceptions to my usual behavior, time will heal it all, and so on."[8]

But true guilt continues to haunt the excuser, and John of the letters (1 Jn 1:8–9) scores this: "If we say, 'we are free of the guilt of sin,' we deceive ourselves; the truth is not to be found in us. But if we acknowledge our sins, he who is just can be trusted to forgive our sins." If I have anesthetized my conscience over some years and boast of not feeling guilty, I do escape painful awareness of my sin (subjective psychological pain) but indirectly the objective effects of my sin linger on like the unwanted side-effects of a pain-killing drug.

Meanwhile the victims of my sins undergo objective suffering (loss of money or reputation or health or hope). Nor do I the sinner, despite my stifled conscience, escape objective suffering since I have degraded myself with dulled sensitivity to others' needs, with shrunken sense of responsibility for my actions, and with lost credibility among those who know my sin.

In contrast, true guilt acknowledged leads to reconciliation with the wronged persons, perhaps in friendship, and to reconciliation with God, maybe in stronger prayer. For it turns attention to the other and to God rather than to oneself. In fact, it enables the sinner to reassess his decisions, to trim his great dream to more realistic expectations,[9] and to turn himself to the sacrament of reconciliation with healthy admission of sin and with stronger purpose of amending his way of life.

Chastened now, I begin to seek God more honestly and to trust more deeply that he never stopped loving me before, during and after I sinned. This approaches a total surrender and shatters the illusion of my independence from God and others. John reassures us (1 Jn 3:18–20): "Little children, let us love in deed and in truth and not merely talk about it. This is our way of knowing we are committed to the truth and are at peace before him no matter what our consciences may charge us with; for God is greater than our hearts and all is known to him."

In stark contrast, false guilt seals one off from God and makes prayer more difficult. Why? Because God cannot console me lest I think my false guilt is true and lose a realistic perspective of life in the fog of false conscience or in the sticky sickness of scruples. As an abused child I am convinced that it is all my fault and that I am thoroughly bad, As a result, later in adulthood, I feel like "damaged goods" unworthy of the spouse and particularly of God. Naturally all my human relationships are fragile and my prayer is falsely guilt-ridden. Furthermore, while undergoing persistent false guilt I become convinced that God cannot love me. Even if God were to tap on the window of my sealed, false-guilt capsule, I would be sure that it is not God tapping since my sins are so ugly and I am so unlovable. This is often the case with the child who, out of mere curiosity, does some sexual experimentation and is punished severely by his startled parents so that, as a result, he enters adulthood still feeling bad about himself. False guilt, then, weakens our spiritual growth and eventually smothers the life out of us.

Lastly, underneath the false guilt, there sometimes lies a smoldering anger against God and others. The falsely guilty person strongly suspects that some injustice is going on somewhere, yet feels that his or her total unworthiness could not dare to challenge God. As anger mounts, a secondary false guilt at having such anger grows. As a result, this guilt-ridden person is less and less able to face God and to pray. It is no mystery, then, why some women are not healthily, but pathologically, angered by the male dominated society and the overemphasis on the maleness of the Christian God. For promoting the anger may well be a twisted false guilt, for example, about having won the affection of the mother from the father and having caused a divorce.

Job absolutely refused to take on the false guilt presented to him by his friends turned accusers (Job 9:29; 13:15; 15:15; 19:6–12; 25:3–6; 27:4–5), and the Lord commended him for this (42:7). For his accusers' false justification of God's seemingly unjust actions toward Job would inevitably lead to false depreciation of Job's goodness and to stultifying false guilt in him. True guilt, then, turns out to be the guardian of our trueness since it enables us to recognize our sins and to repair broken friendships. It further calls us to reach out beyond ourselves and our self-interests even though this is most difficult for us, as St. Paul notes: "I cannot even understand my own actions. I do not do what I want to do but what I hate" (Rom 7:15). Here again, even in true guilt, we meet the anger of frustration smoldering quietly within us. This is why the prayer of anger can be crucially important for us.

D. The Scandalous Prayer of Anger

The prayer of anger rises straight out of one's frustration with one's work (perhaps teaching theology to college students who do not like to read and reflect), out of frustration with one's family or community which seems so oblivious to one's concern for it, out of frustration with one's own fumbling, limited self, and out of frustration with the God whose providence seems to have furnished all these occasions for frustration. The prayer of anger is embarrassing, even scandalous, to a dutiful person because it seems to put him in direct conflict with the God to whom he is praying for help. At times this can fill us with false guilt—unless we recall that our deepest angers are with those we love most. Their lack of attention to us, their thoughtlessness, their lack of confidence in us hurts us in a way that no stranger can achieve simply because our respect for them expects so much more of them.[10]

So, to be angry with God is to pay him the compliment of my love and to let him know how seriously I take his providence and how deeply I trust his affection for me. Once I understand this, I can let my anger become a prayer by facing it literally in the Lord. Finally now, I can search for the cause of this anger, e.g. a false image of God, an unreal and therefore frustrating vision of myself and my talents, a false guilt for a sin that never existed, another's love which is unreasonably demanding of me, my trust of God which requires (contradictorily) a totally satisfying explanation of a friend's unexpected death or of a worldwide famine.[11]

As I now face the problems which God allows to happen in my life, I no longer care whether the dialogue feels consoling or not. I simply want to deal with God about the real agenda of my life, especially the everyday duties of my life. Where I had thought myself lost in a trackless hot desert of anger, I may well have found the path of sanctity.[12] I am letting God be God and discovering his true face.

The prayer of anger paradoxically helps one get over false guilt at being angry toward God—though one could undergo a second false guilt at attempting such prayer unless one had observed the great men and women of scripture who have voiced their anger at God in prayer. The first half of the third lamentation of Jeremiah is so fiercely and cynically angry that it tends to give a person the courage to do such prayer.

Again, Moses twice speaks a forthright anger to God, first while attempting to get Pharaoh to release the Israelites from Egyptian slavery and second when the people were ungratefully rebelling against Moses. On the first occasion (Ex 5:22–23) Moses says: "Lord, why do you treat this people so badly? And why did you send me on such a mission? Ever since I went to Pharaoh to speak in your name, he has maltreated this people of yours, and you have done nothing to rescue them." On the second occasion, in exasperation, Moses asked the Lord: "Why are you so displeased with me that you burden me with all this people? Was it I who conceived all this people? Or was it I who gave them birth, that you tell me to carry them at my bosom, like a foster father carrying an infant, to the land you have promised under oath to their fathers?" (Num 11:11–12).

The prophet Samuel was no different from Moses. He was angry at Yahweh's rejection of King Saul for David.

> Never again as long as he lived did Samuel see Saul. Yet he grieved over Saul, because the Lord regretted having made him king of Israel. The Lord said to Samuel: "How long will you grieve for Saul, whom I have rejected as king of Israel? Fill your horn with oil, and be on your way. I am sending you to Jesse of Bethlehem for I have chosen my king from among his sons" (1 Sam 15:35–16:1).

The Lord is not surprised by Samuel's loyalty to Saul and by his anger at Saul's rejection. This is a good human response, but the Lord does not allow Samuel time to lick his wounds and to grow bitter. He must begin the delicate diplomacy of getting the Israelites to accept David as king.

Jeremiah expresses his anger at what he considers the Lord's trickiness in recruiting him for the prophetic office: "When I found your words, I devoured them; they became my joy and the happiness of my heart. . . . Why is my pain continuous, my wound incurable, refusing to be healed? You have indeed become for me a treacherous brook" (Jer 15:16–18) rising quietly in the night around my sleeping encampment, sweeping me into your turbulent waters, and dashing me against the rocks. He later repeats his charge in a moment of profound depression: "You duped me, Lord, and I let myself be duped; you were too strong for me. . . . The word of the Lord has brought me derision and reproach all the day" (20:7–8).

Job could not be more direct in challenging the Lord with his anger: "How long will it be before you look away from me, and let me alone long enough to swallow my spittle?" (7:18). And again: "God has given me over to the impious; into the clutches of the wicked he has cast me. I was in peace, but he dislodged me; he seized me by the neck and dashed me to pieces" (16:11–12). This is hardly a "nice" prayer.

When Habakkuk speaks out his anger, it is as though he were merely echoing one's own hidden words: "I cry out to you, 'Violence!' but you do not intervene. Why must you let me see ruin; why must I look at misery? . . . This is why the law is benumbed, and judgment is never rendered. Because the wicked circumvent the just" (1:2–4). Jonah wanted revenge on the wicked Ninevites and was chagrined that they were repenting at his call to repentence:

> When God saw by their actions how they turned from their evil way, he repented of the evil that he had threatened to do to them; he did not carry it out. But this was greatly displeasing to Jonah and he became

angry. . . . "Lord, please take my life from me; for it is better for me to die than to live." But the Lord asked: "Have you reason to be angry? . . . Should I not be concerned over Nineveh, the great city, in which there are more than a hundred and twenty thousand persons who cannot distinguish their right hand from their left?" (3:10; 4:1–11).

Jonah hated the Ninevites so much that he angrily begrudged them their reconciliation with God. But the Lord patiently explained himself to Jonah and did not return the anger.

A key characteristic of these angry men and of their prayers is strict honesty; they pray just as they see and feel. Their directness does not allow them diplomatic double talk; they do not dance around the problem and their feeling about it. Rather they plunge into them both by living out the mysteries of their life with prayer of trusting acceptance. They are trusting of God's continuing affection for them no matter what their feelings and words. They have singular hope that God will somehow set things straight even though for the moment he seems to be blundering around. These characteristics keep their prayer from being blasphemous.

By making sure that the feelings and words of his friends were saved for our reading, the Lord invites us to the prayer of anger characteristic of his good friends. Is not such prayer, then, the beginning of the end of our alienation from God? Does not a person risk the anger of a friend out of love because he or she is confident in the perdurance of such love beyond all angers? Does it not seem that the smoldering anger underlying alienation, original and personal sin, and false guilt must be let out if the friendship with God is to grow and perdure? Does all this offer me a fresh image of God, one truer and warmer, more supple and encouraging than I had thought possible?

Chapter Eight
The Joy of Hope:
Response to Alienation

Having explored alienation from many angles, we need to see how its basic cure is the joy of hope. Every previous chapter has ended by describing a prayer-type which arises naturally out of a particular form of alienation. And each prayer turned out to be a practical hoping in God, church, and self. But this is not enough. We need to see the larger picture of hope and its accompanying joy so that we have the courage to live in and beyond the bitterness of alienation.

Possibly because the present world seems to despair of its alienated self, four theologians have taken the lead in proclaiming Christian hope. Calvinist Jurgen Moltmann has expanded the meaning of hope beyond its traditional scope of an individual's salvation.[1] He sees hope as the virtue by which one takes responsibility not simply for one's own future but also for that of the whole world.[2] Lutheran Wolfhart Pannenberg is convinced that the mission of the church is (a) to tell the world that Jesus is the only hope for every person's salvation (b) to actually *be* the community wherein people can live with solid hope in the ultimate fulfillment of humanity and (c) to inspire imaginative social action for bettering the world's life.[3] Hope, then, is seen as strategically necessary. It enables us as individuals and as community to work, with Christ-centered vigor, on troubles which now alienate us from one another.

Among Catholic theologians, Karl Rahner shows how Christian hope is a delicate balance between unreal optimism and dark pessimism: the Christian "is not a person who grasps for something tangible so that he can enjoy it until death comes, nor is he a person who takes the darkness of the world so seriously that he can no longer venture to believe in the eternal life beyond it."[4] On the other hand, Johannes Metz conceives hope as the attitude which frees us from making anything of this world our primary value and which takes God as the sole Lord of the world, the sole absolute worthy of our total love. This attitude, therefore, encourages us to criticize anything less than God in world and church so that both may improve.[5] Here Metz's understanding of hope, by focusing on God as our absolute future, includes the Rahnerian balance. But it also gives us what is necessary for a life dedicated to bettering the church and the world à la Moltmann and Pannenberg.

In accord with this view, Vatican II sees the church as leading beyond passivity by "restoring hope to those who have already despaired of anything higher than their present lot." Indeed, it observes that the church, looking deep into the human heart, calls attention to the dignity of the human vocation, namely, to growing oneness with God and with his people.[6] St. Paul certainly supports these theologians when they stress the importance of hope for the Christian: "Everything written before our time was written for our instruction, that we might derive hope from the lessons of patience and words of encouragement in the scriptures" (Rom 15:4).

All of these elements of Christian hope seem to be contained in the life of the recently canonized Maximilian Kolbe, O.S.F. If any man could have lost himself in the bitterness of alienation, it was Maximilian Kolbe. Many are familiar with the last event of his life when, on July 30, 1941, he substituted himself for another Auschwitz prisoner, one with a young family, and went to a sure and horrible death in a Nazi starvation bunker. What is more remarkable are his earlier feats based on the Christian hope that the mother of Jesus would back his efforts through irresistible requests made to her Son.

First, in the midst of Poland's depression following World War I and despite his own tubercular health (he was nicknamed "marmalade" by some of his fellow friars because of his slow movements), he founded in 1922 a magazine, *The Knight of the Immaculate*. Within five years it reached a circulation of 60,000 and recruited 125,000 members for Kolbe's Militia of the Immaculate. Then in 1927 he began to hand-build in forest-land, along with two Franciscan priests and eighteen brothers and candidates, the City of the Immaculate. Within a decade this community was to grow to 650 conventual friars and candidates and 122 minor seminarians, the largest Franciscan community of men in the world. It was a city composed of a chapel, college, novitiate, friary, and electric plant, and a hundred-bed hospital.

In the midst of this astounding success, hope-filled Kolbe felt that true progress in this city of Franciscans lies "in being poor, without our own resources. . . . If despite all these things the ideal of love and service of God and his Blessed Mother were to grow in our hearts, then, my little children, we can say we are in full progress."[7] Then, to the surprise of all, in 1930 Kolbe left the City of the Immaculate with four brothers to found a similar city in Nagasaki, Japan. Within one month, with the help of a Methodist minister and a Japanese university professor, Kolbe published the first Japanese edition of *The Knight*—despite the fact that soliciting subscriptions was against Japanese tradition and could not be done. Within four years the community swelled to twenty-four members and within six years twenty Japanese were studying for the priesthood within the Franciscan Order.

In 1936, Kolbe, frequently hemorrhaging from tuberculosis, was summoned back to Poland to attend the general meeting of his community. Once there he was told by his superiors to remain in Poland at the City of the Immaculate. By December 1938 he had put Radio Niepokalanow on the air and had begun planning an airport and sending several brothers to Warsaw for pilot training. Meanwhile his undaunted hope was dreaming about using television for evangelization. But the Nazis' 1939 invasion of Poland cut short his work and led to his imprisonment and martyrdom. His remarks to Dr. Joseph Stemler, another prisoner, summed up neatly the hope which energized him. Stemler recounts how "he helped me to strengthen my belief in the final victory of good. 'Hatred is not creative,' he whispered to me. 'Our sorrow is necessary that those who live after us may be happy.'"[8]

Bruno Borgowiec, a fellow Auschwitz prisoner assigned to

remove dead bodies from the starvation bunkers, recalled: "When I was about to carry the body of Father Kolbe out of the cell and opened the door, I noticed that he was sitting on the floor leaning against the wall. . . . His body was most clean and radiant. . . . His face was bright and serene. The bodies of other prisoners I found lying on the floor, begrimed, with faces betraying signs of despair."[9] Could it be that Kolbe's radiant body and bright serene face are the symbol of his living that Christian hope which the four theologians described and which alone ultimately protects us from bitter alienation?

Here is a man achieving future victory out of a ravaging tuberculosis, out of a financial depression, out of a forest floor, out of the stifling restrictions of a foreign country, and out of a Nazi concentration camp. His hope was not merely for his own life, but it entered creatively into the hearts of all who worked with him, giving them strength to do and to suffer whatever he did and suffered. He once remarked to his friar friends: "I hope that after my death nothing remains of me, and that the wind blows away my dust over the whole earth"—so much did he love and hope in this world and in its creator.[10] Perhaps we could look at how such hope feels in order to recognize its presence in our own lives.

1. The Feel of Hope in Our Lives

Paradoxically, the very challenges to our hope reveal it stretching within us to meet these challenges and to control our fear of failure. When a person is fearfully sweating through a decision to take on a risky venture (a financial gamble for the family's sake or the confronting of a friend and his alcoholism), she may discover a secret strength, even a certain deep-down joy, for following through on this decision. This hope also rises in a person when he meets the huge contemporary problems of worldwide disintegration of family life or nuclear warfare or international terrorism or third and fourth world financial debacles capable of pulling down the first and second world economies. Somehow Christian hope says to him: "This is God's world; he will see to its survival; he loves it more than you do. So, do your small bit to keep the world going and perhaps even to improve it infinitesimally."

At another time, hope may express itself within us as a strange sense that something grand awaits us. This can occur when a person is under severe pressures, even during break-down in work and life. It requires a great faith-leap into the foggy future.[11] Wordsworth's "Lines Composed a Few Miles Above Tintern Abbey (1798)" expresses this hauntingly:

> . . . And I have felt
> A presence that disturbs me with the joy
> Of elevated thoughts; a sense sublime
> Of something far more deeply interfused.
> . . . A Motion and a spirit, that impels
> All thinking things, all objects of all thought,
> And rolls through all things.

A second way to isolate my feeling of Christian hope is to contrast my power-desires with the vulnerability of my hope. In my desire for dominance, my possessions can become more important than my own being and cold reason can constrict my sense of wonder. When empowered, I aim to master or control my family, business, local politics, church, and even leisure sports. There is need to achieve total security from loss. This is accomplished by running everything with neat rules which fail to take into account emotions, attitudes, sufferings, and mys-tery. Consequently, my competitive spirit and my envy rule over my cooperativeness and compassion. People are, there-fore, valued for what they can produce as useful experts, not for what they are as human beings. When this raw ambition takes over in a whole nation, it inevitably produces conflicting factions like labor versus management or the wealthy versus the poor or the educated versus the uneducated. Such ambition is, then, the bad seed causing vast alienations and poisoning the smallest joys.

In direct contrast to this is the feeling of vulnerability at the heart of hope. Here the wonder of mystery is more impor-

tant to me than the carefully reasoned accumulation of possessions. I place more value on the mystery of a person than on
what he or she owns. But when I respect the unpredictable
mystery of life by allowing another person to be utterly free or
by trusting others' cooperation out of compassion for their previously slavish plight, I risk my comfortable security. Hope
involves danger because deep respect for others as well as acting out of faith in God's providence can at times prove costly in
betrayal and sorrow. Does not my hope then stretch thin and
the result of my decision become severely painful? On other
occasions, however, this same hope can make the threatening
event endurable and the dreaded surrender to the beloved's
needs both possible and gladdening.[12]

A third discovery within one's experience is that hope is a
sense of the resurrection beginning to occur in one now, not
just later after death. It is the feeling that all alienations will
finally end sometime and that oneself and the community will
be completely healed for the fullest of lives. This is experienced
when one's work for the kingdom outdistances one's abilities,
opportunities and even dreams. The very practical St. John
Neumann would never have envisioned himself building in
Philadelphia the first of all the American parochial school systems. But his hope taught him to gamble the finances of the
whole church of Philadelphia during depression time to build
that system.

Again, Mother Cabrini, young, inexperienced and in poor
health, could hardly have foreseen her newly founded order
expanding so swiftly to work successfully in Europe and in both
the Americas with such large numbers of Italian immigrants.
But she learned how to gamble on God's providence and on the
goodness of all the people from whom her sisters begged funds
for hospitals and schools—often at taverns on Friday paydays
and on the streets of poor urban areas. When Pauline Jaricot,
partially recovered from teenage paralysis, began to form her
"circles of ten" among the low-paid seamstresses and silk workers of Paris, she had no idea that her "prayers and pennies"
program for the China missions would become the Society for
the Propagation of the Faith with a global outreach to Asia,

Africa, and Latin America. But her hope made her an inveterate gambler living from one tight situation to the next. Very likely these three gamblers felt deep within them the secret joy of hope in God and others. Then this hope led them to expand their reconciling work far beyond any small boundaries they had first set.

This sense of the "now" resurrection is also frequently found in the continuous joy of everyday hard work on behalf of others—this continuity being another aspect of that radical prayer discovered earlier.[13] Ignatius Loyola illustrates this. Here was an aggressive soldier-type urged by a secret deep joy to climb a mountain of correspondence which detailed the problems, scandals, and occasional successes met by his men. This deep hope surfaced in his *allegro* eyes and in his frequent heart-warming laugh which encouraged his men greatly when they visited him in his office.

Such an attitude of joyful hope was equally present in Francis Xavier who, in the dead of the Japanese winter, would keep warm by throwing an apple high in the air and racing along under it to catch it. His lyrical voice and, again, his dancing eyes once converted two Portuguese traders whose spoken language he did not know; he used another language, that of a heart filled with hope in Christ and others. The deep joy of his and Ignatius' hope, actually the presence of the Holy Spirit within them, not only united these two close friends in daring action but reached out to give joy to others. One of the reasons for the success of their work was the continuousness of this joyful hope within their daily tasks. For joy lends us both energy and strength ("The joy of the Lord is your strength"—Neh 8:10), just as the bitterness of alienation, after the first violent thrust of revenge, saps our energy and leaves us weak with ennui.

Such hope is most manifest in one's illnesses and sufferings when one finally recognizes that they are opportunities to reduce the level of suffering in the lives of others. For, in learning what pain is in our own bodies and hearts, we know like Christ how to lessen people's minor and major agonies with practical compassion, with gentle humor, and with the evidence of our own joyful hope in God and others. In a world of so much suffering, this secret, underlying joy can become continuous.[14] It may be found even on a death-bed as one Bavarian Jesuit superior discovered. He had just admonished a dying elderly lay-brother for not taking death more seriously. The brother replied: "Whose death is this, yours or mine? Besides, I'm going to a great homecoming; that's what my parents told me when I was a child." The joy which the brother felt was his hope, the beginning of the resurrection in his very death. But what is the source of this joyful hope that heals all alienations?

2. The Fact of Hope Being Fulfilled

A. Joy Growing in Christ's Heart Out of Our Hope in Him

To get underneath the cliché that Christian hope is vitalized in us by Christ's resurrection, we should note the actual process by which the heart of the risen Christ inspires our hope in him and each other.[15] But four principles must first be laid down to establish this explanation:

1. What distinguishes the human being from all infrahuman beings is that the human never stops growing, whereas infrahumans like the beasts hit a final plateau of development and then start declining. (Even the person hit by arterial sclerosis of the brain, while handicapped greatly in thinking, can still grow in grateful affection for others.) Because human personality growth, then, is what constitutes the human being, it will continue as long as we are human, that is, long after one's earthly death.
2. This unlimited human growth is what makes the human being a human and not merely an animal. Jesus, the finest of humans, would naturally grow forever in his human nature or personality. This is *not* his unchanging and perfect divine nature of which we speak. Rather, our focus is on his human personality which is composed of his human body and soul with their powers of sensation, emotion, thought, and willing. Christ's human personality would also include all his

developing virtues, emotional sets, knowledges, and imaginative schemata which together hold the total *human* experience of Christ's personal cumulative history.

3. Christ's heart, then, stands for his developing human personality with its depth of compassion. It is not simply his physical organ called the heart; it is much more. It is his human personality which, in all its facets, has been steadily growing for almost two thousand years.

4. Like all growth of the human personality, Christ's human growth is through interchange with others such as his Father, the Holy Spirit, the angels and, last but not least, us humans. In other words, just as he changes us with his thoughtful care (called grace), so we change him with our intelligent affection shown him in our daily activities and in prayer and liturgy. Also, when we give joy to his beloved people by serving them in their needs, we increase the joy in his heart since he takes delight in the happiness we give to others. For he himself spent his life giving joy to his Father by giving joy to the Father's people (the woman with the hemorrhage, the apostles in the upper room, the blind man Bartimaeus leaping with happiness at his cure). In fact he left a trail of joy behind him at the great expense of brain-deadening fatigue, constant tension, poor food and lodging, and eventually his life-blood. This did not happen by chance, he informs his disciples; but "as the Father has loved me, so I have loved you. . . . All this I tell you that my joy may be yours and your joy may be complete. This is my commandment: love one another as I have loved you. There is no greater love than this: to lay down one's life for one's friends" (Jn 15:10–13).

With these four principles in mind, one can see how the risen Christ is the final source of our hope. He lures us on by the attractiveness of his compassionate human personality to make costly decisions for him and his people. Then, as St. Augustine has noted, [16] Christ assists us with the insights, the courage, and the imaginative creativity necessary to carry out these decisions for him and his people. His great heart, standing for his warm human personality, is, then, the source of our hope and of our relief from bitter alienation. For the risen Jesus' humanity compenetrates ours to live his life within our very beings, within all our actions.

B. The Growth of the Christian's Heart Out of Hope in Christ

To understand the hope within us, it is not enough to know how Christ's heart expands with joy inside our beings and throughout our actions. We need to know how our own hearts grow large with joyful hope. St. Paul puts it neatly: "He comforts [strengthens] us in all our afflictions and thus enables us to comfort those who are in trouble with the same consolation [joy] we have received from him" (2 Cor 1:4). By accepting suffering into our own hearts, we can pass on Christ's accompanying strength to make it easier for others and to bring some modicum of happiness into their hearts. Clearly, one cannot do this without hope in the future, Christ's future. The more children a mother has, the more she can expect suffering. The more risky the venture which a CIA agent undertakes for his country the more sure he is of failure. Counselors find themselves totally at the mercy of their clients' decisions even though they have done not much more than listen, inform, and make gentle suggestions. How move into such vulnerability without a strong conviction that Christ lives now and is providing for one's future?

Acceptance of vulnerability by parents or public servants or counselors, then, becomes the mark of Christian hope. Not without risk does one attempt to help others to find some happiness, by luring them into reconciliation with themselves and others. St. Paul, nevertheless, urges us to this work: God "has reconciled us to himself through Christ and given us the ministry of reconciliation. . . . He has entrusted the message of reconciliation to us. This makes us ambassadors for Christ, God as it were appealing through us" (2 Cor 5:18–20).

Only strong hope enables us to resist all the evils of the world and to surrender to no one of them because of despair over their cure. In the face of their mammoth size, it would be so much easier to surrender to financial servitude of the third and fourth worlds, to abortion on demand, to the general subordination of women to men, to vast unemployment among displaced peoples, to enrichment of the wealthy with money extracted from the poor, and so on. It is difficult to accept being called Don Quixote by person after person. Yet Christian hope encourages us never to give up on these huge problems, nor on our smaller personal alienations.

If we can relieve only a small part of others' sufferings, we move closer to the heart of Christ. Indeed, we give others and him much more than a modicum of joy since the slightest relief expresses personal love and stands for tomorrow's hope. Meanwhile for those who have not given up, life can contain a quiet continuous joy which tends to flow through each one's entire twenty-four hour day. Besides, as nurses, social workers, parents, and religious workers know, there is no end of people who need strengthening joy to be given them day after day.

Such deep and persevering compassion, because it demands strong faith in God's providence and in Christ's leadership, is explainable only by a Christian hope. Providentially, sickness or psychological breakdown or utter failure in family life can end up in hope and compassion. In desperately trying to escape our troubles, we fall into God's helping hands as our only final hope. Paradoxically, despair of self has rendered us utterly open to God who then can reward us with himself and with a core conviction that life has ultimate meaning. This experience of hope can then be exported to others if they are receptive.

For example, once while giving a thirty-day retreat to young priests (with a sense of utter failure) and facing the imminent death of my mother, I went through five sleepless nights, praying that God would take me immediately. This event made no sense to me until some months later I received a midnight call from my cousin a thousand miles away, asking me to give her one good reason for not swallowing the heap of sleeping pills held in her hand. From my five suicidal nights I knew what not to say and how to persuade her to wait till I flew to her side. My own hope, newly discovered amid suicidal thoughts, enabled me to arouse some hope in her.

On another occasion at a retreat house, I overheard the lay-retreat organizer telling the retreat-house director that their retreat master would not be able to come the next week because of an emergency operation. So, I jauntily volunteered to substitute. The retreat organizer replied: "Thanks, Father, but really we need a priest alcoholic." The priest suffering from alcoholism had, in a paradox of grace, become the beacon of Christian hope for others aching to escape addiction.[17] What had been alienating was being transformed into reconciliation by this hope.

There is a second reason why the persevering compassion for others finds its ultimate explanation only in Christian hope. After all, hope is Christian not only because it is caused by Christ within us but also because in his total vulnerability he lived such compassion himself for our encouragement. During his Palestinian life he too felt vulnerable and he needed, as no one else in all history, solid hope in the Father's providence. For example, he was exulting in his baptism because of the Father's warm approval of him and because of the Spirit's descent on him. But within a short time, his heart would become exhausted as he struggled with the three temptations. Each temptation suggested that he put more trust in his own powers as the Christ and less hope in the Father's affectionate providence for him. Yet out of this terrible event came his ability to encourage us during our desolating temptations both by his example and by his graceful enlightenment of our darkness.

Again, after he had been warmly greeted in Nazareth by his old friends and kin, and had entered his favorite synagogue to pray and preach, he experienced, with sinking heart, his fellow Nazarenes' crippling lack of faith. Seemingly cut adrift by his own people, he felt homeless, discouraged and defeated when he slipped out of Nazareth. He needed hope to continue on to Capernaum and make it his new home. Yet out of this came his ability to heal our alienations from family, our feelings of homelessness, with his example and with his graceful attention to our stubborn hurt.

There are other gospel-instances of how his own felt need for hope amid vulnerability enabled him to better minister to our need for hope. In John (6:60–69) we discover Christ wondering whether anyone will accept his self-gift in the eucharist. Already some of his close disciples have left him because of scandal at his generous vulnerability. So, he asks the disciples: "Do you want to leave me too?" Out of this abandonment, out of this feeling of hopelessness, issues his knack for companioning us in our desperate times with a song of hope. Even after his ascension, if we take seriously the revelations of St. Margaret Mary and the writings of Bl. Claude de la Colombiere, the risen Christ still experiences in his vulnerable heart the coldness of rejection and the warmth of our devotedness. His heart, then, still experiences increase of joy and the emptiness of rejection. Even now he knows what the feel of reconciliation and alienation is.

It is in the dark experience of death, however, that one can discover the sharply contrasting brightness of joyful hope already present in one's exhausted body and tired spirit.[18] For the dying person already begins to feel a new closeness to the material world as her soul anticipates entry into the very core of the universe where God is.[19] She has a premature sense of the reunion of her body with a newly enspiriting soul. No longer is her person to be cramped by the narrow limits of the body once given her in conception. Through this more supple resurrected body and through her freer spirit, she will join the new world of her friends, the community of saints surrounding Christ. This is the secret anticipatory joy of the dying person who has hope.

But her hope is even more profoundly enlarged by the slowly dawning realization that God loves all peoples, not just Christians, and wants all dividing alienations between nations and people healed as Isaiah indicated (19:25). The God who creates all things (and particularly human beings) loves them individually, spares them, and is present in each and all of them (Wis 11:22–26; 12:1). For this reason, Sirach tells us, the works of God are all of them good (19:33). Indeed, God penetrates each human heart (42:18) and as a result we see how beautiful are all his works (42:23). So let the last word be: he is all in all, the reconciler in all reconciliations, and yet he is far greater than even all these works (43:28–29). This can be the experience of the dying person whose life has been hopeful. In this way God's very being and all his works move toward this final reconciliation, this final embrace, between the dying person and all beings. This is our hope in God's omnipotence, providence, and goodness as he works to end all alienations.

Thus, our own ministry of hope to others, our witnessing of Christ serving us out of his hopeful vulnerability, and finally our sense of God's encompassing care during our dying hours convince us of one fact: our reconciling compassion for others' needs is rooted in Christian hope. We are trying to live Peter's advice: "Venerate the Lord, that is, Christ in your hearts. Should anyone ask you the reason for this hope of yours be ready to reply but speak gently and respectfully" (I Pet 3:15). Our own experience of Christian hope becomes the best source of hope for others. This brings us to the question: What could be our faith-response to this marvelous gift of Christian hope?

3. Joyful Glorification of God: Our Faith-Response to the Lord's Gift of Hope

A. *Joy Is the Distinguishing Mark of the Christian Apostolate*

Carlo Martini, cardinal archbishop of Milan, gives us pause when he says: "Whenever we are not completely happy, it means that there is something, some conditioning, hindering us even though we may not speak about it or admit to it."[20] This may explain why Benedict XIV's two-volume outline of the canonization process uses the first third of the first volume for explaining how to explore the evidence for the potential saint's sense of joy. If such joy is missing, then there is no need to continue the process; the person is simply not a canonizable saint.[21] Without joy, there is apparently no hope; without hope, there is apparently no faith; without faith, how can charity operate?

This is reasonable since Christian joy comes from confidence that Christ is the rescuer in all our sorrows, sufferings, and defeats and is the sponsor of all our ambitions, successes and joys. For this reason, a Christian's meditations on death and suffering in his own, others' and Christ's life are a source of joy rather than of pagan depression. For "who will separate us from the love of Christ?" (Rom 8:35–39) which gives us profound joy. Indeed, "God is greater than our hearts and all is known to him" (I Jn 3:20), and so we are confident that he continues to cherish and aid us whether or not we are in sin, in sorrow, and in suffering. Because forever faithful, he is our ultimate source of hope in our great future.

Depression rises, however, when one is convinced he has a poor future. Actually when alienation is allowed to continue unchallenged in one's life, a subtle despair begins to work against one's hope. The resultant depression is basically the loss of joy. Then when one's despair begins to deny all future joy, suicidal thoughts start to occupy the forefront of one's consciousness. One sees the world's problems as hopelessly huge and complicated and oneself as a foolish one-time optimist.

In sharp contrast to this defeatist attitude, the "third degree of humility" in the Ignation Exercises[22] suggests that a great lover of Christ will *prefer* to be with Christ dishonored in his poor and to be thought a fool rather than to be with the honored and those considered wise. Though this preference is mistakenly dreaded by some as a frightfully inhuman demand, the "third degree of humility" is simply another way of saying: "As often as you did it for one of my least brothers, you did it for me" (Mt 25:40). Such humility is a graced privilege (not a ruthless demand) because it offers the secret joy of hope in Christ and in his anawim. This joy assures those working for faith and justice that God takes delight in their sacrifices for his abandoned ones, the born losers. Thus the "third degree of humility" is meant to dispel any depression and to restore the joy of hope in one's life and in one's work for the disadvantaged of the world.

In such a context, this joy becomes the criterion for judging whether or not an apostolic life is truly Christian and not simply social activist.[23] Did not the angels herald to the outcast shepherds the joy of Christ's birth in stark poverty? Did not the early Christians express the Easter joy in their faces and in their charitable deeds to the bitterly cynical pagans watching them die in the Coliseum? Should not joy, then, rather than harsh zealotry characterize Christian activism if it is based on Christian hope? Further, the dour Christian who bitterly grouses over social problems and offers little help for their alleviation offers witness to something quite other than Christian hope and joy. In losing the joy of hope, has he not lost the creative energy to do more than wring his hands, voice recriminations and discourage others?

B. Why Is Joy the Basic Criterion for Truly Christian Living?

How could joy be the touchtone for estimating the reality of one's Christian living? A faith-response to this question contains the following principles. First of all, Christ's resurrection is not merely something that happened back there two thousand years ago, simply an historical event like Caesar's crossing of the Rubicon. Christ's resurrection was the dawn of heavenly life for the whole pagan world of the first century. With noontime radiance, it is still radiating out through the twentieth century and is, as always, giving the whole world a sacred destiny—an insight which threads all the writings of Teilhard de Chardin.

Second, the risen Christ is within each of us. His immortal body, soul and existence compenetrate the body and soul of each of us to form his mystical body. In other words, all his personal richness rests at the center of our being, waiting to be released through our creative decisions. He is the Lord of history not merely as guiding it to its future destiny but also as containing cumulatively all the experience gathered through his two thousand years of interchange with the whole human race. He recapitulates all the nobility, beauty, and truth of the universe within his human personality. No person, no generation, has failed to add a unique contribution to this richness.

Here is Wisdom itself, the Christ, residing in each of us and waiting to be given to others through our laughter, our hands, our compassionate intelligence, our eyes, our labors and the joy of our face. This presence of the risen Christ, our reassuring joy, cannot be taken from us by anything or by any persons;

only we in our freedom can give it away. Thus the joy of Christ's ongoing resurrection, the sure basis for Christian hope, can be seen as an ultimate criterion for judging the worth of Christian life.[24] As Léon Bloy, the French novelist, puts it: "Joy is the infallible sign of the presence of God."

There is a third reason for claiming that joy is a basic criterion for estimating Christian life. Even before our resurrection, we are an "earthly heaven" for all our beloveds and they for us. For our comradeship includes a persistent hope in each other and in the perdurance of our friendship through all time. Yet this hope (and our joy in it) would be empty if there were no God to assure its future—a vibrantly living God who not only supports this comradeship but also is the friend of friends, the shaper of all communities and the fountain of all joy. Indeed, this is what heaven after death becomes: the grateful community of comradely saints glorifying God while Christ joyfully enfolds them into the Trinity-family.

Thus our earthly search for God can be the richest of gifts for our friends. It is our response to the Lord's timely creating of us out of nothing. We labor through the growing years so that we can eventually reach a "forever being with God." Here is the ultimate mysterious meaning of history: as the world evolves toward deeper union with God over millions of years of dire trials, monstrous mistakes and occasionally brilliant successes, this Christian evolution turns out to be the better and better imaging of God in all creatures, especially in man. For a person's growing joy in her life gives her the energy and strength to live a fuller and fuller human existence.

This increase of her humanness becomes, then, the better imaging of God's intelligence, freedom and beauty of life. Julian of Norwich, a fourteenth century English mystic, is a humorous, earthy lady who thinks of prayer as "homely dalliance," of spiritual direction as "full merry counsel," of English religion as "full boistrous," of the ambiguities of life as "marvelous mix-up," of the pleasure of redemption as giving "joy" to the Father, "happiness" to the Son, and "eternal delight" to the Spirit.[25] Certainly Julian's delight would be the final embracing of her God who takes such pleasure in creation and especially in herself. Does this not portray Christian hope and life in its most appealing guise?

Genesis, then, has rightfully described the delight God took in his creation which, by his omnipresence, he witnessed from beginning to end with one glance. Through Christian hope, God can share this delight with us and we can offer it to each other at every hour of our life as the personal and communal history of humans evolves toward God. Such joy, stabilizing all sufferings, pains, and even death, can become, then, not only an indicator for the direction of one's life but also an ultimate criterion for measuring one's union with God in the here and now.

For example, during the Korean War, a contingent of American soldiers and their chaplain, Fr. Emil Kapuan, a diocesan priest, were overrun and captured. The long journey back deep into the interior of North Korea was a nightmare of stinging blizzards, rock-like rutted roads, and twice-a-day cold rice with occasional mugs of lukewarm tea. Some would have given up had not the chaplain cajoled, shamed and strong-armed them. They found the prison camp even worse than the road as their unexercised limbs stiffened with the cold and the food proved scarce—so scarce that Fr. Kapuan developed ingenious techniques for stealing food from the guards for the sick and weakest.

Meanwhile, some noticed that he ate very little himself so that his face became gaunt and his eyes seemed piercing in their deep sockets. But there was a strange resemblance to someone in his face and the soldiers began to call to him: "Hey, Christ, come over here—this guy is dying; hey, Christ, hiding any food for us?" Only a lethal attack of pneumonia froze the warmth of his eyes and throttled his laugh. Even in death he continued to smile. His joy in the midst of hell was unforgettable to these soldiers. Could such joy be the growing awareness of the Spirit's presence at the center of Kapuan's being as he quietly fitted friendships and acquaintanceships into the mystical body? This is heaven on earth subtly underlying even agonies of suffering, giving direction to one's life and deepening one's union with the Lord. It is reconciliation at its worst and at its best.

On this basis, one can see why the celebration of Christ's death and resurrection in the eucharist becomes a raising up of the whole magnificent world to the majestic Trinity through Christ. It is one grand act of worship as we experience both joy and sorrow simultaneously and yet "celebrate" since joy is forever, while sorrow is time-bound. Significantly, the risen joyful Christ is the center of the liturgy. St. Paul notes: "It pleased God to make absolute fullness reside in him and, by means of him, to reconcile everything in his person, both on earth and in the heavens, making peace through the blood of his cross" (Col 1:19–20). Here is our joyful hope in daily living dramatized unforgettably.

The young Jesuit seminarian, John Berchmans, would understand this. For even while haunted by the thought of an early death during Rome's bitter winter, he continued to study for the grand examination conducted before the Roman cardinals and continued to show visitors around Rome with such graciousness that chance passers-by inquired about this young man with the bright smiling face. Berchmans knew how to celebrate his hopeful joy in the crucified Christ amid worry, fatigue, and the pressure of studies. It played a leading role in his celebrating the eucharist of reconciliation.

But out of this, a fourth reason rises for saying that joy is an ultimate criterion for Christian living. After all, what is heaven but God's definitive closeness to us in our day-to-day living whether at work or liturgy or play or suffering moment? Philip Neri understood this as few others did. He was a great puzzle to proper priests as he stood at a street corner in Rome, listening and telling jokes to young men and women. Even more puzzling was his arrival at a fashionable gathering with the right side of his beard shaved off to poke a little fun at the partying dandies and their ladies. Meanwhile the less proper poor and youth of Rome learned that joy was an important part of life even as they confessed their sins to Neri and joined him in founding a new order of religious dedicated to helping the helpless find some dignity in themselves. For Philip Neri God and his heaven were to be found on the street corners of Rome and in the hovels of the poor, to say nothing of fashionable parties.

Still, even after death and after entering into the Trinity's family, we will continue to seek God. For he is infinitely beautiful and desirable, always new to our seeking even as we hold him. In this way our joy is forever. But it is hardly boring since it is renewed each second both in us and in the human personality of Christ himself. Does not our own glory, that is, our own fullness of being, end up glorifying his glory, his infinite being? This is a question, as we shall now see, whose partial answer shows the magnificence of human destiny.

C. *God's Glory on Earth Is the Joyful Christian Community*

God's glory on earth and the dawning of his kingdom are remarkably similar. Richard McBrien defines the present ongoing kingdom of God as "the redemptive presence of God actualized through the power of God's reconciling Spirit."[26] By accepting this graceful presence of God within us and by letting it issue out through our en-Spirited actions into the world, we become resplendent human beings since God shines through our actions without our ever quite knowing this. "For God who said, 'Let light shine out of darkness,' has shone in our hearts, that we in turn might make known the glory of God shining on the face of Christ" (2 Cor 4:6). Like all pioneers, Katherine Drexel, the Philadelphia heiress of the Drexel banking family, was informed how futile were her enterprises for two lost causes, the New Orleans African-Americans and the Albuquerque Indians. But her face, though lined with cares and tired from all-night train travels in dusty coaches, still shone with hope; and her actions, aglow with interest in her people, gave them hope to struggle for the full dignity of their lives. For, as Irenaeus tells us, the human fully alive is God's glory.

We so reveal God's glory within us (and thus alert others to his kingdom) in four ways. First, by simply being called by Christ (to our and others' surprise). "It was not you who chose me; it was I who chose you . . . out of the world" (Jn 15:16–19). The call energizes us into full life, into full glorying in our God-given dignity, into the enthusiasm of sacrifice for others. In this way, we naturally end up glorifying God, that is, gracefully drawing the attention of others to his goodness.

Second, when we later labor for others in harmony with fellow Christians and with the Spirit of Jesus, we call attention to the Lord's encouraging presence among people and in events. This helps people to recognize his delicate care of them and to respond in gratitude; they glory in him.

> Each should please his neighbor so as to do him good by building up his spirit. . . . May God, the source of all patience and encouragement, enable you to live in perfect harmony with one another according to the spirit of Christ Jesus, so that with one heart and voice you may glorify God, the Father of our Lord Jesus Christ. Accept one another, then, as Christ accepted you for the glory of God (Rom 15:5–7).

Third, when Christians consistently put others first, people become curious about the source of such constant and costly generosity. They wonder why Christians are so hopeful of them and why Christians are so willing to suffer for the world. Paul answers their question: "We boast of our hope for the glory of God. But not only that—we even boast of our afflictions! We know that affliction makes for endurance, and endurance for tested virtue, and tested virtue for hope" (Rom 5:2–4).

Fourth, by following Christ's lead and not dodging the sufferings which are necessary to make the world a little bit happier, we clearly state in action that this world is our home; we own it. "But if we are children of God, we are heirs as well, heirs with Christ, if only we suffer with him so as to be glorified with him. I consider the sufferings of the present to be as nothing compared with the glory to be revealed in us" (Rom 8:17–18) because "the present burden of our trial is light enough, and earns for us an eternal weight of glory beyond all comparison" (2 Cor 4:17). Our glory becomes our willingness, because of hope, to suffer for others' sake in order that they may find the Lord in their daily life and praise-glorify him for his protective goodness to them.

In these four ways, we literally become God's glory (his full life in us) and eventually found the final kingdom "the full and perfect manifestation of the redemptive presence of God through which all things are transformed in the name of Jesus Christ and by the power of the Holy Spirit."[27] This kingdom is our hope, the source of our joy, the élan of our glorying in God: "So may God, the source of hope, fill you with all joy and peace in believing so that through the power of the Holy Spirit you may have hope in abundance" (Rom 15:13). Here it becomes clearer how God's glory shining in our joy has its source in our Spirit-given hope.

John the evangelist's description of the last supper (Chapters 13–17) brings this glory of God shining in us down to everyday living. To glorify God is (a) to obey his commandments just as Christ followed the Father's commands (15:8–12), (b) to love one's fellow Christian even to death—as Christ did (15:12–13) and (c) to be one with each other as Christ is with the Father (17:22–24). Indeed, it is in and through us that Christ himself is being glorified (17:10) because we are living as he does in glorifying the Father.

And so, one naturally feels the joy of Christ in oneself (16:20–22). For our joy is to love one another in the way Christ loves us (13:31–35; 15:12–17;17:23–26). Then, since we accept all God's gifts in order to use them for others (16:12-15), we are glorifying the God in Christ. In return gratitude, Christ loves us as the Father has loved him and we live in this love by keeping Christ's commandments just as he kept the Father's commandments (15:9–11). Of course, this means that we will endure the hate of the worldly just as Christ did (15:18–27; 17:14–18). Yet at the very same time we will share in Christ's joy as he gives his suffering people the taste of eternal life, namely, affectionate knowledge of the one true God and his Christ (17:1–3, 24–26).

The glorification of God, then, consists in giving joy to his heart by letting his glory be resplendent in our actions for others and in our very being. The wise man speaks for Yahweh: "My son, if your heart be wise, my own heart also will rejoice and my inmost being will exult. . . . My son, give me your heart and let your eyes keep to my ways" (Prov 23:15–16, 26). This analogy becomes a direct reality when the heart of Christ, his whole personality, is expanded by our joyous love for him and by our hope in him shown through our Christian actions. To glorify Christ is to expand his heart with our confidence in him just as conversely the lack of confidence muffles the heart's generosity, verve, ambition, and ingenuity. Reciprocally, too, the glorifier, in failing to glorify, robs himself or herself of joy and of heart-expanding generosity.

All this joy and expansion of heart in the one glorifying and in the one glorified is actually reconciliation with God as one's heart identifies with his joy and hopes. It is also reconciliation with others insofar as they unite with us to form the mystical body of Christ out of love for God. In fact, it is also reconciliation with God's whole universe when each part of it is seen as capable of giving joy to us, to others, and to God. This results in self-reconciliation since there is no longer any reason for self-recrimination.

We now see what St. Paul's Colossians came to understand: Christ's reconciliation of the world is God's glory. Therefore, "it pleased God to make absolute fullness reside in him and, by means of him, to reconcile everything in his person, both on earth and in the heavens, making peace through the blood of his cross" (Col 1:20). The full horror of alienation now becomes evident. It divides and distances disastrously the self, one's friends and family, one's whole world. It veils the splendid caring face of God and makes him hard to experience when actually his glory is dawning with splendor behind the clouds. This is something of the obscure immediacy of God to all we do and are.

In contrast, full reconciliation unites all the orders of the universe into one great order and turns our gratitude to God into his increasing glory. For we are home in our Father's universe. This Paul indicates: "Everything is ordered to your benefit, so that the grace bestowed in abundance may bring greater glory to God because they who give thanks are many" (2 Cor 4:15). Fittingly he ends his letter to the Romans with a doxology which indicates that the glory given to Christ becomes the Father's glory: "Now to him who is able to strengthen you in the gospel which I proclaim when I preach Jesus Christ . . . to him, the God who alone is wise, may glory be given through Jesus Christ unto endless ages. Amen" (Rom 16:25–27).

To put this more simply, the joy which one helps others experience is precisely God's glory in them and implicitly their giving of glory to God. The helper, in turn, gives glory to God. For when this helping expands the helper's joy, she or he becomes a living glory to God. Further, this glorying is the joy-filled reconciliation between the helper and the one helped. In addition, any joy given to another is joy given to the heart of Christ who, in turn, gives thanks to the Father. This gratitude of Christ becomes the Father's glory. Thus to give joy to another is to glorify Christ, the Father, the other person, and oneself in a single simple act.

But none of this could happen unless one had a deep hope in self, the world, Jesus Christ as redeemer, and God as the loving creator of the universe. And no person could do this alone without God's help. Paul notes this clearly:

> It is by grace that you have been saved, through faith; not by anything of your own, but by a gift from God, not by anything you have done, so that nobody can claim the credit. We are God's work of art, created in Christ Jesus to have the good life as from the beginning he had meant us to live it (Eph 2:8–10).

But how does a person, after becoming aware of these basic facts about hope, joy and God's glory, learn to live them? One way is to do Trinity-prayer.

4. Trinity-Prayer—Contemplation To Attain Divine Love

This Trinity-prayer is a glorying in God and his creation. But it is done concretely within one's personal experience; it is not a philosophical musing or a general grocery-listing of God's gifts. One focuses, within the imagination, vivid lively pictures of faces, places, and events in detail. This assures the contemplator of some emotional response; after all, we are dealing with hope, joy, and glory, not with architectural plans or vague vistas. Here are some ways of doing this Trinity-prayer.

As you look at the *triumphant* Christ on the cross, repeat the name of Jesus softly while focusing this name on each one of your anxieties, emptied hopes, sins, and fiascos. If you are doing this prayer with Christian hope and with the desire to give Christ glory, over a time you will experience him gradually working reconciliation within your being and body. He is slowly liberating you from fear, bitterness, and fallacy so that you can experience some joy in yourself. This joy, no matter how subdued or muffled, is your glorification of Christ. This glory he will, in turn, give to the Father so that in giving glory to Christ you are simultaneously glorifying the Father. This is reconciliation in all its beauty. "For God who said, 'Let light shine out of darkness,' has shone in our hearts that we in turn might make known the glory of God shining on the face of Christ" (2 Cor 4:6).

Later, picture your friends, one by one; and while viewing each one, speak the name "Befriender" to the Holy Spirit who has, with great care, united you now to this friend and later to that friend and lastly to still another friend. For the role of the Holy Spirit is to build the body of Christ out of such friendships. Even review, one by one, the faces of acquaintances, of students or of patients whom you serve, and breathe the name "Befriender" again and again over each one. These are the people, along with the Holy Spirit, in whom we place hope and from whom comes our joy. So, after this Trinity-prayer, St. Paul's words may carry additional meaning: "May God, the source of hope, fill you with all joy and peace in believing so that through the power of the Holy Spirit you may have hope in abundance" (Rom 15:13).

Finally, picture the Father gifting you from minute to minute with life. Feel your pulse, at once the gift of energy and the symbolic fact of mortality. Then repeat "Father" as you slowly enjoy the faces and scenes surrounding each gift received: family life of parents-brothers-sisters-aunts-uncles-cousins, health (specific instances of hospital stays, visits to doctors, tests indicating fitness), education (teachers, wise counselors, study-successes), worthwhile work (jobs held, awards received, failures felt, people helped), vocation (skills and knowledges developed, times of disciplined sacrifice, sense of mastery) and future hopes (marriage, children, service to the needy, recognition for work done and for friends made). What becomes more evident to us in this Trinity-prayer is that "God makes all things work together for the good of those who have been called according to his decree. . . . Those he called he also justified; and those he justified he in turn glorified. What shall we say after that? If God is for us, who can be against us?" (Rom 8:28–30).

This Trinity-prayer illustrates how God has glorified each of us with joy flowering out of each one's love for friends-family-world-self and out of God's love for these same people. This happens as he heals each of us from the alienations experienced in family life, work, prayer, community rivalry, career competition, and crippling fears. Trinity-prayer can alert us to Father, Son and Spirit graciously operative in our world and self so that competition becomes minimized and facilitation of others becomes maximized. These very healings or reconciliations turn out to be joyful and to be God's glorying within us. Slowly we are becoming his living image, his living glory. For this reason, hope in self, others, Jesus Christ, the Holy Spirit, and the Father is so basic, so vital, to one's total present and future life with them. Such hope is the ultimate source of joy in this world of ours. It is the basis for all reconciliation.

Epilogue: The Dynamics Between Types of Alienation-Prayer

It is easy enough to see the ties between the various types of alienation coming out of one's work-situation or family-life or disaffection from God or lack of self-esteem. But it is much more difficult to note the dynamics between the various types of prayer which arise out of these situations. Perhaps a few clarifications on this point would be of help.

It is good to recall that the basic aim of *Healing the Ache of Alienation* is to achieve awareness of the obscure immediacy of God—right in the midst of temporary alienations from others, self, and God. Obscure immediacy refers to the *almost direct* experience of God that can be had in these seemingly hopeless situations. The immediacy is there in all one's daily actions, but recognizing it is not always easy. If it were, this book would be unnecessary. Nor is this recognition without some complexity. For one must focus a number of insights and feelings accurately in order to see and feel the immediacy. Thus come the long lists of factors frequently offered in this book so that one can zero in on the experience of a particular type of alienation-prayer.

Further, because the factors are experiential, the searcher for this immediacy must take time and care to isolate them. Nothing can substitute for this quiet reflection on one's prayer experience—which reflection happens to be a praying. Naturally, these procedures take for granted that one has been praying faithfully over some years so that he or she has something to reflect upon.

This obscure immediacy, if described theologically, is, of course, grace arising in one's experience. To put it another way, it is God's presence coursing through one's spirit and central nervous system; it is a growing union with him. Indeed, it is reconciliation with him and his people. Such immediacy is deepened by healthy alienation from the world, by acceptance of one's limitations, by sorrow for sins, by trust in the Father's unique providence for oneself, by companionship with Christ, and by the joy of the Holy Spirit uniting one with all the members of the body of Christ through the sacraments. This immediacy is, on the other hand, threatened by unhealthy alienations from the self, the world, God's people, and the one Lord of all. Finally it is brought to full and direct experience through one's death, purgatory and resurrection. Then all obscurity vanishes.

This obscure immediacy of God's presence during our earthly existence takes many forms according to the situation in which it rises. Nevertheless the resultant diverse types of prayer are interrelated since they all express in different ways the union of the individual person with the one God and Lord of all. Besides, the prayer of trust is the basic type underlying all other kinds of prayer and strengthening them.

Because trust prayer is so fundamental and is so prevalent in all other types of prayer, it is hard to describe. Rather, it is simply done out of a serene confidence that "I am loved, lovable and loving in the midst of my sins and shortcomings." The "old shoe," in reconciling others, can experience alienation in his or her self and yet know a secret joy, a persistent hope in the final reconciliation of all people. The "old shoe's" actions contain the compenetrating warmth of the Holy Spirit dwelling deep within each reconciler. He is the living promise of the great tomorrow.

This trust prayer is lived by way of radical prayer which, implicit and hidden in each person's life and actions, generates the mysticism of service and of Christian solidarity. Radical prayer starts with the questioning-wondering prayer. For the latter is a reaching into mystery, a fumbling for God's presence in baffling happenings, a beginning of trust within mysterious natural events but also a moving far beyond them. It is the first uncovering of the depths of God's affection for us.

Then radical prayer grows more honest through prayer of anger. The person praying through a questioning-wondering finds himself or herself angry at the frustrations of life and lashes out at the provident God. Though this anger-prayer appears to be a direct challenge of God, it actually contains a deep respect for him. Only the one we trust and love can goad us to such burning anger. God is not horrified at this conflict. After all, alienation is a basic ingredient of life, as the Bible demonstrates, and will naturally appear in prayer—if one is honest with God.

Through this honesty, radical prayer is established within the "prayer of community." For now the praying person more realistically appreciates the sacraments, especially that of reconciliation. He or she discovers objectively that Christ identifies with us sinners and builds his family, the church, around each one of us to give us a home—we are only as alone as we want to be. As this objective reconciliation occurs, one's subjective acceptance of this reconciliation begins to ripple out from one's center and to encircle close friends, the family, the parish, the world of nature, and the human universe. One deeply respects God, the world, and others and consequently respects oneself. Here the mysticism of service becomes stronger.

In this way, radical prayer moves into self-respecting body prayer of simply mute gestures, then of words and gestures, and finally of gestures, words, and actions. Such prayer, deepened by the self-knowledge which comes out of suffering and sorrow, then prepares one for the wisdom process. There are no shortcuts to wisdom. Through the four stages of contemplation, one comes to that analytic contemplation whereby one finds God more objectively in each thing and event and to that synthetic contemplation whereby one more subjectively contextualizes all things and events in the presence of the Lord of history. Thus one peers deeply into a particular event and yet at the same time sees the event in its cosmic situation. As a result, this wisdom prayer eventuates in wise actions which embody simultaneously love of God and of neighbor. Here radical prayer becomes a serene and powerful contemplation-in-action.

But radical prayer is now tempered by frustration-peace prayer, a blazing fire of loyalty within the wisdom process. Frustration-peace prayer helps one to resist factual alienation from God's presence even when feeling terribly alienated. It demands therefore that one grow in the presence of God and recognize by interior and exterior criteria that one is loved dearly by God even though one experiences various dark nights. It gives a peace beyond mere sensual satisfaction, pleasurable joy, and beatific self-fulfillment. This peace is nothing less than a continuous sense of being right with God. Such an experience focuses radical prayer sharply on the obscure immediacy of God within one's every action and situation.

Lastly radical prayer is crowned by Trinity prayer, the beginning of everlasting life, the commencing of the final reconciliation of all one is and has with the divine All. Here, because of the growing sensitivity to the immediacy of God, a rather constant underlying joy is experienced in hour-to-hour living amid all the shifts of life. This fuller Christian life is, therefore, the touchstone for evaluating Christian experience. It is a glorying in Christ as one's faithful brother. It brings one to full manhood and womanhood, the basic aim of the Father's continuous creative act within the developing human person. This glorying is a compound of self-respect, of the giving of joy to others, and of hope in the Trinity. As one focuses one's joy on Christ, he glories in the fact of one's reconciliation and carries this joy to the Father. Here one learns, in glorifying the three persons of the Trinity by name and with gratitude, that each is glorying in oneself. This becomes a dynamic contemplation for attaining the love of God and for serving him generously as one ministers to all those who will accept one's embrace and find Christ there. This forming of the kingdom becomes an anticipation of the last alienation and the final embrace when all who wish are united to each other in Christ so that they may immerse themselves as God's people in the full Trinity-family.

Appendix: Alienation Prayers
in the Ignatian Spiritual Exercises

It would seem that the various alienation prayers delineated here could be useful at different stages of the Spiritual Exercises of St. Ignatius.

The prayer of questioning-wondering (Chapter Five) might well enter into the principle and foundation at the beginning of these Exercises—especially after one has employed the prayer of reminiscence to uncover one's personal salvation history with all its heartaches and gifted moments. Does not the recovery of one's lived history lead into questioning and wondering?

Then, too, in the first week or stage of the Exercises the prayer of anger (Chapter Seven) could bring the retreatant to fuller honesty in dealing with those alienations and attitudes which rise during the outset of the retreat to badger the retreatant and discourage any hope of conversion. At this juncture the retreatant badly needs the "prayer of community" (Chapter Four) to know that he or she is not alone but is accompanied by the family of God, especially fellow-retreatants amid confusions, troubles, joys and everyday sacramental living.

As one enters the second week or stage of the Ignatian Exercises, the prayer of Christ's memories can make Christ more palpable to us, while the prayer of the body (Chapter Three) not only puts one at ease with one's own body but leads one to accept more fully God the Son's incarnation. Then the wisdom prayer, at its imaginative-sensuous and aural-insightful levels (Chapter Three), can become operative as one reflects on the kingdom, the two standards, and Christ's public life.

The third level of wisdom prayer, namely radical prayer (Chapter Two), can now be focused on the passion and death of Christ in the Ignatian third week or stage. At this point the prayer of listening described in my *Radical Prayer* enables one to assume a more passive observation of the passion. At the same time the prayer of frustration-peace (Chapter Six) enables one to deal with the scandal of the cross in Christ, family, community and self, while it uncovers the basic peace of the resurrection already occurring in Christ's and one's own passion.

During the fourth week or stage of the Exercises, the prayer of the Trinity (Chapter Eight) opens the retreatant to an intensely personal appreciation of God's provident love. Then the fourth level of wisdom prayer, contemplation-in-action, arises to challenge one to reply to this love of God for each of us. As St. Paul put it: *Caritas Dei urget me.*

Notes

Introduction

1. *Habits of the Heart* (Harper and Row, New York, 1986, pp. 275–296).

2. *Time* (Feb. 2, 1987, "Economy and Business," pp. 49–55) describes graphically the decline of quality in the service industries and hints at the individualism causing this decline.

3. George A. Aschenbrenner, S.J. defines the bridge-building needed to span the "Quiet Polarization Endangering the Church" (*Human Development,* Vol. 7, #3, 1986, pp. 16–21). He traces much of the polarization to overly ideological thinking and then profiles the qualities needed in the bridge-builder.

4. Gerard Egan and Michael A. Cowan in their *People in Systems, a Model for Development in the Human-Service Professions and Education* (Brooks/Cole, Monterey, Calif., 1979) give a concise description of this social demoralization and see it as possibly day-to-day alienation (pp. 1–3). They also offer an understanding of the four-stage cycle of human behavior (perception < attention < transformation < action) which can be quite helpful in analyzing and dealing with alienation (pp. 24–40).

5. *Modern Dictionary of Sociology* (Thomas Y. Crowell Co., Apollo edition, 1961, p. 9). John Lachs (*Intermediate Man,* Hackett Publishers, Indianapolis, 1981, pp. 20–21) strongly cautions us about the use of the term alienation. He has three problems with it: (1) its basic vagueness, (2) its inclusion of both the subjective element of feeling and the objective event causing the feeling (is it relation or process or product?), (3) its inclusion of both notion and value without revealing the underlying premises for the value judgment. As we proceed through the following chapters, an attempt will be made to avoid these pitfalls.

6. One gets some idea of how widespread alienation is from

Robert Nisbet's remark (*The Sociological Tradition*, Basic Books Inc., New York, 1966, pp. 264–312) that the concept of alienation began with Descartes though its recognition as a scientific term started in the nineteenth century. There the individual was viewed as uprooted, alone, estranged from places-work-self, and bereft of uniqueness. There, too, modern society was viewed as inaccessible because of its remoteness, heavy structure of organization and impersonal complexity. Alienation becomes, then, the opposite of what progress and individualism had promised to achieve through their subversion of tradition. Toqueville saw the resultant secularism as the diminishment of humaneness. The sociologists were horrified when they observed the unbalanced rationalization of reality (Weber), the human isolation and *anomie* (Durkheim), and man's fragmentation into roles, his loss of identity, his inability to socialize (Simmel: "the metropolis is a city of strangers") because all these factors were causing alienation across the whole western world.

7. John Kavanaugh, S.J., *Following Christ in a Consumer Society* (Maryknoll, New York, Orbis, 1981).

8. Quoted in *The Word Remains: A Life of Oscar Romero* by James R. Brockman, S.J. (Orbis Books, Maryknoll, N.Y., 1982, p. 73). This biography quietly lets the facts speak with their own powerful eloquence about Archbishop Romero's life.

9. In *Sacred Discontent, The Bible and Western Tradition* (University of California Press, Berkeley, 1976), Herbert N. Schneidau includes a chapter called "In Praise of Alienation" where he states: "In philosophic terms, what the Bible offers culture is neither an ecclesiastical structure nor a moral code, but an unceasing critique of itself. For this critique a certain cost must be paid: we habitually call this cost 'objectivity,' but its original name was alienation." This would be a prime example of healthy alienation.

1. Alienation from "My World"

1. In his *Clives Staples Lewis, A Dramatic Life* (Harper and Row, San Francisco, 1986, p. 240) William Griffin quotes C.S. Lewis' description of this terror of exclusion.

2. Ladislaus Boros, *Pain and Providence*, translated by Edward Quinn (Baltimore, Helicon, 1966, p. 79). Boros goes on in the following pages to indicate how selflessness, gratitude and vulnerability play major roles in the joy of a Christian. He even states: "Nothing makes the Lord so sad, even wounded in soul, as a Christian who does not live in joy" (p. 80).

3. *The Eternal Year*, translated by John Shea (Burns & Oates, London, and Helicon Press, Baltimore, 1964, p. 132).

4. *St. Francis of Assisi, Writings and Early Biographies: English Omnibus of the Sources for the Life of St. Francis*, edited by Marion A. Habig (Franciscan Herald Press, Chicago, 1972, pp. 465–468).

5. For the best documented life of Archbishop Oscar Romero consult the neatly written *The Word Remains: A Life of Oscar Romero* by James R. Brockman (Orbis Books, Maryknoll, N.Y., 1982). *Romero: A Life* (1989) is a second edition expanded with new material from his spiritual notes and his pastoral letters.

2. Work: Source of Alienation and Solidarity

1. Studs Terkel in his book *Working* (Avon Books, New York, 1975, p. xiii) puts it well: "[This book] is about a search, too, for daily meaning as well as daily bread, for recognition as well as cash, for astonishment rather than torpor; in short, for a sort of life rather than a Monday through Friday sort of dying. Perhaps immortality, too, is part of the quest. . . . There are, of course, the happy few who find a savor in their daily job." This remarkable book of interviews carries in it inexpressible yearnings for nobility of life alongside partially withered hopes.

2. John C. Haughey, S.J., "Civilizing Work" (*America*, May 9, 1987, pp. 382–384).

3. *Pastoral Constitution on the Church in the Modern World*, in *The Documents of Vatican II*, Walter M. Abbott, S.J., editor (Guild and America Press, 1966, chap. 4, #42, pp. 241–242).

4. Chap. 1, #2, pp. 491–492; cf. also chap. 2, #5, pp. 495-496, in *The Documents of Vatican II*, Walter M. Abbott, S.J., general editor (Guild and America Press, 1966).

5. Cf. the four-page *Catholic Update*, "Lay Catholics Today: 'We've Arrived,'" by Barbara Beckwith, under the general editorship of Jack Wintz, O.F.M. (St. Anthony Messenger Press, Cincinnati, August, 1987, CU 0887) for a very compressed yet rich digest of the latest thoughts on the lay apostolate. Many practical suggestions are included.

6. *The Pope in America II*, The Addresses of Pope John Paul II During His Second Visit to the United States, September 10–19, 1987 (Wanderer Press, St. Paul, 1987, III, p. 88).

7. "When Jesus Said 'No,'" *The Catholic Life Series* (Archdiocese of Los Angeles, Liturgy Commission, 1531 W. Ninth Street, Los Angeles, CA, 90015, 1981).

8. In his "United States Technology and Adult Commitment" *(Studies in the Spirituality of Jesuits*, Vol. 19, 1987/1, pp. 26–34), John M. Staudenmaier, S.J. suggests that the crisis of America's technological culture has brought us to a state of confused commitments, standarized motives, a lost vision, and, above all, a crying need for intimacy.

9. See Henri Daniel-Rops, *Daily Life in the Time of Jesus*, translated by Patrick O'Brian (Servant Books, Ann Arbor, 1980, pp. 146–148).

10. See "On Human Work: A Reflection," by Rev. David A. Boileau (*Blueprint for Social Justice*, Vol. XL, 1986/4) where he digests neatly John Paul II's philosophy and theology of work.

11. The notion of solidarity achieved through the mysticism of service is not something far removed from the workaday world as some may think. Robert K. Greenleaf, retired Director of Management Research for A.T.&T. and now a widely employed business consultant, in his *Servant Leadership* (Paulist Press, New York, 1977) insists that soon individuals will be chosen as leaders "because they are proven and trusted as servants" (p. 10). This applies especially to churches and not merely to other institutions such as business concerns, universities, government bureaus, and foundations. For "the dynamics of leadership—the vision, the values, and the staying power—are essentially religious concerns and fostering them should become the central mission of the growing edge churches." These should "add to their historic mission of caring

for persons and to their more recent regard for the social order, the mission of caring for institutions" such as those just mentioned (p. 81). This is the servant leadership of church leaders and of the people of God since "businesses, despite their crassness, occasional corruption and unloveliness, must be loved if they are to serve us better" (p. 136). Such service will happen only if the business institution is seen as also including a community of workers whose "work exists for the person as much as the person exists for the work" (p. 142). Then trust will exist in the institution, will make it lovable and will render it eager to serve others well. This will engender trust in the people served by the institution. For "the only sound basis for trust is for people to have the solid experience of being served by their institutions in a way that builds a society that is more just and more loving" (p. 70). Such an institution arises, therefore, only when its members feel that their work and they themselves are meaningful because of good service to the commonweal. This provides the sought-for solidarity of the civil body and of its spirit, the servant church.

12. See *A Theology of Christian Prayer*, by John H. Wright, S.J. (Pueblo Publishing Co., New York, 1979, pp. 122–125) for fuller development of this theme.

13. "Since Christ in his mission from the Father is the fountain and source of the whole apostolate of the church, the success of the lay apostolate depends upon the laity's living union with Christ. . . . Only by the light of faith and by meditation on the word of God can one always and everywhere recognize God, . . . seek his will in every event, see Christ in all men whether they be close to us or strangers, and make correct judgments about the true meaning and value of temporal things, both in themselves and in their relation to man's final goal." Decree on the Apostolate of the Laity (*The Documents of Vatican II*, Guild and America Press, New York, 1966, p. 493).

14. In my *Radical Prayer* (Paulist Press, New York, 1983, pp. 5–19) and in my *Dark Intimacy* (Paulist Press, New York, 1986, pp. 94–99) these four levels of prayer experience are developed further.

15. Richard P. McBrien describes this fundamental option in his *Catholicism* (Winston Press, Minneapolis, 1980, Vol. 2, pp. 954–957).

16. See James Carroll's *Prayers from Where We Are* (George A. Pflaum, Dayton, Ohio, 1978).

17. This is well described with an attached bibliography by Caroline McGinn, S.C., in her "Reaching for the Unknown" (*Contemplative Review*, now known as *Living Prayer*, Vol. 19, 1986/1, pp. 9–14).

18. Michael Mott in his *The Seven Mountains of Thomas Merton* (Houghton-Mifflin Co., Boston, 1984, p. 7) quotes a letter of Merton describing his prayer: "It is centered entirely on attention to the presence of God and to His will and His love. That is to say that it is centered on *faith* by which alone we can know the presence of God . . . it is a matter of adoring Him as invisible and infinitely beyond our comprehension . . . there is in my heart this great thirst to recognize totally the nothingness of all that is not God."

19. Thomas H. Green, S.J. speaks of "floating prayer" as leading into fuller and fuller trust of God as the Lord of one's life whereas most of us have been struggling to swim to God with much self-reliance. See his *When the Well Runs Dry* (Ave Maria Press, Notre Dame, 1978, pp. 142-151).

20. See "Praying Our Experience," by Joseph Schmidt, F.S.C., 1980, a booklet distributed by him from Christian Brothers Conference, 100 De La Salle Drive, Romeoville, Ill., 60441-1896. The original articles appeared in *Benedictines*, Vol. 23, 1978/1 and 2, pp. 19–25, 48–54, 70–78, 115–118; the quotation is from p. 19 of the original article.

21. These points of measurement are modified from my *Radical Prayer* (Paulist Press, New York, 1983, pp. 74–77).

3. *Healing of Body and Spirit in Wisdom*

1. For this particular theme I am indebted to the suggestion of Sr. Janet Schumacher, P.B.V.M. of Aberdeen, S.D.

2. Anthony de Mello, S.J. has written three very popular books to encourage bodily prayer: *Sadhana: A Way to God,*

Song of the Bird, Wellsprings: A Book of Spiritual Exercises (Image-Doubleday, Garden City, N.Y., 1984–87).

3. In recent talks the psychologist Douglas Heath has cautioned us about the validity of the "midlife crisis" as a predictable developmental stage in the average person's life.

4. See his *Spiritual Direction and Midlife Development* (Loyola University Press, Chicago, 1985, pp. 40–47) whose content I have modified to suit the purposes of this section.

5. Prayer of reminiscence and prayer of Christ's memories are described in my *Radical Prayer* (Paulist Press, New York, 1983, pp. 20–50).

6. This type of prayer is described in Chapter Five, Part II, of this book, pp. 86–91.

7. The prayer of listening is outlined in my *Radical Prayer* (Paulist Press, New York, 1983, pp. 51–61).

8. See Chapter Two, Part 3, of this book for the description of radical prayer.

9. I have tried to explain concretely what apostolic contemplation-in-action is in my *Radical Prayer* (Paulist Press, New York, 1983, pp. 62–80), and in my *Dark Intimacy* (Paulist Press, New York, 1986, pp. 53–86). I also detailed the experience of the "more" of purification in this same contemplation-in-action.

10. I am using this distinction between these two types of contemplation-in-action and some descriptions of them as found in *A Theology of Christian Prayer* (Pueblo Publishing Co., New York, 1979, pp. 94–95) by John H. Wright, S.J.

11. Could these stages of contemplation actually be the conversion process described by Bernard Lonergan in his *Method in Theology* (Herder and Herder, New York, 1972, esp. pp. 237–244)?

He speaks first of an intellectual conversion where a person turns from a merely self-world to the world as it really is. In this way he moves out of alienation from the world to reconciliation with it by way of love. Then comes a moral conversion when the person, recognizing the self as free and responsible, starts to make decisions based on values rather than on mere personal satisfaction. This brings reconciliation with the self out of a sense of dignity or self-respect. Finally there is religious conversion where the person becomes a being totally in love with God—with all his or her heart, mind, soul, and bodily strength. This is manifested in love for neighbor since reconciliation with God and world always results in reconciliation with one's neighbor.

12. See *The Divine Milieu* (Harper and Brothers, New York, 1960, p. 110) as quoted in Richard P. McBrien's *Catholicism* (Winston Press, Minneapolis, 1980, p. 1073).

13. See his *The Inner Search* (Sheed and Ward, New York, 1957, p. 7) as found in McBrien's *Catholicism*, p. 1074.

4. The Deepest Wound

1. See Henri Nouwen's *Intimacy* (Harper and Row, San Francisco, 1969, p. 29).

2. Richard P. McBrien gives a useful definition of Christian asceticism as what is "concerned with those 'exercises' which help us to regulate the conflict between the spirit and the flesh. It involves painful struggle, self-denial, and renunciation. It is the acceptance of one's facticity and the historical limitations of one's existence. Patterned on the cross, asceticism is obedience even to the point of death and leads to the service of others" (*Catholicism*, Winston Press, 1980, p. 1010; cf. also pp. 986–988). Spirituality is, of course, the motivation which directs asceticism.

3. Few more eloquent pages about God's love for us and about our problem in accepting this love can be found than in *As Bread that Is Broken* by Peter G. van Breemen, S.J. (Dimension Press, Denville, N.J., 1974, pp. 9–35).

4. C.S. Lewis once delivered a sermon on the basic flaw in one's life and strongly recommended confession for its alleviation or at least a written list with a serious act of penance for each item. "A serious attempt to repent and really to know one's own sins is in the long run a lightening and relieving process," he thought (*Clives Staples Lewis, a Dramatic Life*, by William Griffin, Harper and Row, San Francisco, 1986, pp. 253–254).

5. Of course this is an applied use of the "Prayer of Reminiscence" described in my *Radical Prayer* (Paulist Press, New York, 1983, pp. 20–37).

6. What is said here about confession is usable for the daily examen of consciousness to render it alive with new discoveries and to enable it to delve into the mysterious presence of God and self at the depths of one's being.

5. *Joseph of Nazareth's Alienation from Mary*

1. The major portion of this chapter appeared as "Impertinent Questions Put to Joseph, Husband of Mary," *Sisters Today* (Vol. 54, 1983/7, pp. 413–415) under the editorship of Sr. Mary Anthony Wagner, O.S.B.

2. On April 12, 1977, the Father General of the Society of Jesus, Pedro Arrupe, spoke in Madrid to representatives of the major religious orders in the Catholic Church. His speech was entitled: "What New Challenges and Opportunities Face Religious Life and Our Experience Today?" (translated by Daniel F. Hartnett, S.J.). Fittingly, his title ends with a question mark as he speaks of our sense of mystery (pp. 6–8) and states: "The question is a sign of our times . . . [as we] experience God imprecisely, more along the lines of mystery than as proof and assurance." This remarkable talk attempts to sketch the future of religious experience from the contemporary problems and needs of modern society.

3. My attempt to sketch what this prayer of listening and waiting may be is "Prayer of Listening-Waiting," *Sisters Today* (Vol. 53, 1981/4, pp. 208–215). A later version of this appears as Chapter Four of *Radical Prayer* (Paulist Press, New York, Mahwah, 1983).

6. *The Loneliest Experience: Mid-Life Divorce*

1. This chapter comes out of the accounts given me by some married women and men suffering divorce and by some men and women religious undergoing alienation from their communities. It is *not* the author's attempt to hypothesize how

women or men must feel in such circumstances. Particularly helpful in criticizing this chapter were Elizabeth Drugan, S.H.C.J., Marcia Lunz, O.S.F., Linda Therese Strozdas, S.S.C., Mary Anne Hoope, B.V.M., Theodore Tracy, S.J., Edmund Fortman, S.J., and John Dillon, S.J.

2. In his *Spiritual Direction and Midlife Development* (Loyola University Press, Chicago 1985, pp. 40–47) Raymond Studzinski, O.S.B., has intricately woven together the latest literature on midlife crisis and spiritual direction to give us a wise overview of a complicated situation.

3. Marie Conn, I.H.M., "The Loneliness of Transition," *Review for Religious* (Vol. 45, 1986/2, pp. 293–295) and "Transition: A Bridge," *Sisters Today* (Vol. 53, 1982/8). Anne Steinacker, S.S.N.D., "Transfer: A 'Second Journey' Experience," *Review for Religious* (Vol. 45, 1986/6, pp. 914–921).

4. "What New Challenges and Opportunities Face Religious Life and Our Experience Today?" A speech given by Pedro Arrupe, Father General of the Society of Jesus, in Madrid, on April 12, 1977, and translated by Daniel F. Hartnett, S.J., pp. 4–5.

5. For a much fuller description of these four levels of experience, confer my "The Fourth Level of Prayer: Mystery," *Review for Religious* (Vol. 39, 1980/6, pp. 807–820). This is also Chapter One of my *Radical Prayer* (Paulist Press, New York, 1983). See also my *Dark Intimacy* (Paulist Press, 1986, pp. 94–97).

7. Smoldering Anger at God

1. Much of this section comes from the description of Ladislaus Boros' *Pain and Providence*, translated by Edward Quinn (Helicon Press, Baltimore, 1966, pp. 19–27).

2. I am indebted for much of the organization of this section to Richard McBrien's *Catholicism* (Winston Press, Minneapolis, 1980, pp. 162–165).

3. In Isaiah (46:11 ff) a concept of corporate sin can be inferred since Yahweh intends to free the Israelites as a nation

from their group exile, a common punishment for their sins, through the agency of Cyrus, the Persian emperor.

4. Pierre Grelot, "Faut-il Croire au Peché Originel?" *Études*, Vol. 327 (1967), p. 233. In the consideration of original sin, the dissertation and scholarly guidance of the Rev. Alec J. Wolff, priest of the Archdiocese of Chicago was of indispensable help.

5. We are talking here of the medieval *potentia obedientialis* or of Rahner's supernatural existential as elaborated by Richard McBrien in his *Catholicism* (Winston Press, Minneapolis, 1980, pp. 160–161).

6. On this important point confer David Hassel, S.J., *Searching the Limits of Love* (Loyola University Press, Chicago, 1984, pp. 165–169) where I endeavor to show how it is impossible to observe one of Christ's two great commandments without observing the other. Cf. also Pierre Rousselot's "Pour l'histoire du problem de l'amour au Moyen Age," *Beitrage zur Geschichte der Philosophie des Mittlealters* (Bd vi, Hft. 6), a textual study of Thomas Aquinas' theory of disinterested (other-centered) love in terms of part and whole. He works with these texts: In II *Sent.*, d. 1, q. 2, a. 2, resp. and *Contra Gentiles*, III. 24 and 25. Benjamin Llamzon explores this same phenomenon philosophically in his *The Self Beyond* (Loyola University Press, 1973, pp. 86, 119–134).

7. A remarkably condensed and concise article on guilt, "Guilt . . . and What To Do About It" has been published by *Christopher News Notes*, 12 East 48th St. New York, N.Y. 10017, May 1984.

8. See C.S. Lewis' *Problem of Pain* (Macmillan, New York, 1975, Chapter Four) for his analysis of this sin-denial.

9. Sean D. Sammon ("Growing Up Guilty in America," *Guilt: Issues of Emotional Living in an Age of Stress for Clergy and Religious*, edited by Kathleen E. Kelley, Affirmation Books, Whitinsville, 1980) contends that constant reflectiveness on one's behavior is necessary for trimming one's great ambition or dream to a more realistic project which will integrate one's skills and render one's life more wholesome. The alternatives are to give up one's dream or to refuse to trim it back to reality. Both these latter procedures produce depression and guilt.

10. Patrick M. Closkey, O.F.M. tells us in *When You Are Angry with God* (Paulist Press, New York, 1987) that the admission of anger toward God will not lead to agnosticism or atheism but will usually enable us to pray. Its denial, however, may well result in a lifeless belief in God.

11. *May I Hate God?* by Pierre Wolff (Paulist Press, New York, 1979) analyzes the feeling of hate toward God and lists all the good people of scripture who prayed over such hate with God.

12. J.P. De Caussade, S.J. in his *Abandonment to Divine Providence* (B. Herder, St. Louis, 1921, translated by Dom Arnold, O.S.B.) sees sanctity as "fidelity to the duties appointed by God" and "its passive exercise consists in the loving acceptance of all that God sends us at each moment" (p. 3).

8. The Joy of Hope

1. In his *Summa Theologica* Thomas Aquinas describes quickly (II-II, qq. 17–22) how the individual's will is elevated by grace to expect eternal life and the means to its attainment. See Richard P. McBrien's *Catholicism* (Minneapolis, Winston Press, 1980, pp. 699–701, 973–975) for the source of my remarks about hope.

2. *Theology of Hope* (New York, Harper & Row, 1967).

3. *Theology and the Kingdom of God* (Philadelphia, Westminster Press, 1969, pp. 74, 83–85).

4. *Foundations of Christian Faith* translated by William V. Dych (New York, Seabury Press, 1978, p. 405).

5. *Theology of the World* (New York, Herder and Herder, 1969, pp. 107–140).

6. *Pastoral Constitution on the Church in the Modern World*, n. 21 (*The Documents of Vatican II*, ed. Walter M. Abbott, S.J., New York, Guild and America Press, 1966, p. 220).

7. *Maximilian Kolbe* by Boniface Hanley, O.S.F. (Notre Dame, Ave Maria Press, 1982, pp. 45–46). This compact booklet, filled with revealing pictures and striking text, is my source.

8. *Ibid.*, p. 65.

9. *Ibid.*, pp. 71–72.

10. *Ibid.*, p. 72.

11. See Ladislaus Boros, *Pain and Providence* translated by Edward Quinn (Baltimore, Helicon, 1966, pp. 65–66). In his *Will and Spirit* (San Francisco, Harper and Row, 1982) Gerald G. May speaks of the "unitive experience," a self-losing awareness wherein one feels caught up in a suspended moment. One is totally wide-awake and open; everything is experienced with awesome clarity; worries and desires evaporate and leave everything seemingly perfect (p. 53). Usually one recalls this event with "a sense of having had a momentary insight of things as they are and were meant to be" (p. 64). The implicit desire for self-surrender is no longer a problem but becomes the wellspring of one's deepest hope (p. 2). Though this experience is somewhat rare, we all seem to have had it along life's journey. Could it be the highpoint of the virtue of hope?

12. Many of the leads for this paragraph and the preceding one were furnished by James P. Grace in his article, "A Philosophical Basis for Abandonment" (*Spirituality Today*, pp. 234–241) where he develops Gabriel Marcel's basic attitude toward life (the valuing of being over having) as a foundation "for the radical demands of the Christian way of life" (p. 237).

13. See Chapter Two, Part 3, of this book for a fuller discussion of what radical prayer is and how it can be recognized.

14. See Boros, *Pain and Providence*, pp. 54–55.

15. For a fuller explanation of how Christ's human nature or personality can continue to grow after his ascension into heaven, see Chapter Seven, "The Secular Christ," in my *Radical Prayer* (Paulist Press, New York, 1983).

16. See the ending of St. Augustine's dialogue, *The Teacher*.

17. See Boros, *Pain and Providence*, pp. 52–55, 64–69, for some of the key insights of this section.

18. See Boros, *Pain and Providence*, pp. 46–51, for the source of these insights.

19. See Boros, *Pain and Providence*, pp. 46–51, for the suggestions of hopefulness in this section.

20. Carlo M. Martini, S.J., *Through Moses to Jesus* (Notre Dame, Ave Maria Press, 1988, p. 51). Martini holds that the fundamental evil is the inability "to effectively practice love of

God and especially love of neighbor . . . in responding to the actual situation of the neighbor's need even where the person does not deserve our help, is not worthy of it." Failure here, he says, results in dissatisfaction, uneasiness and disgust. Of course, the opposite of this is Christian hope ministering to desperate people.

21. See Benedict XIV, *Opera*, 5 vols., edited by J. Silvester (Prato, Italy, 1839–47).

22. I have endeavored to demonstrate that the "third degree of humility" is the pivot of the entire Spiritual Exercises of St. Ignatius, expresses the heart of the gospels, and strongly supports the social apostolate in Chapter Eight of *Radical Prayer* (New York, Paulist Press, 1983).

23. See Boros, *Pain and Providence*, pp. 8–9, 28–31.

24. *Ibid.*, pp. 28–31.

25. Elizabeth Dreyer offers a tantalizing sketch of Julian of Norwich in her article "Julian of Norwich: Her Merry Counsel" (America, August 5, 1978, pp. 55–57).

26. See McBrien's *Catholicism*, vol. 2, p. 1102.

27. *Ibid.*, p. 1104.